Betty Crocker's Chocolate Cookbook

Betty Crocker's
Chocolate
Cookbook

PRENTICE
HALL
PRESS

New York London Toronto Sydney Tokyo Singapore

Think chocolate! Here is a feast of memorable recipes to gladden the hearts of dedicated chocolate lovers. This comprehensive but discriminating collection ranges from the best time-tested classics like Hot Fudge Sundae Cake to new taste delights such as Chocolate Terrine and Chocolate Mousse Cake.

There are recipes for pies and cakes as simple as Banana-Peanut Pie and as fancy as Hazelnut Chocolate Torte; cookies including an all-time winner, Chocolate Chip, and scrumptious Caramel Candy Bars. Old favorites such as Rocky Road Fudge compete for favor with rich, creamy Truffles and Chocolate Apricots.

Desserts range from puddings and cheesecakes, crêpes and cream puffs to fruit and meringue creations to sigh over. Think warm Chocolate Soufflé with rich Creamy Sauce or easy but elegant Chocolate-dipped Strawberries on a cloud of whipped cream. Ice creams, tortes and rich chocolate sauces are not forgotten, either.

An introductory section includes a history of chocolate and expert advice on choosing, storing and melting it. Easy yet creative decorations such as chocolate curls, leaves and cut-outs are also included. And beautiful color photographs throughout show just how your finished chocolate fantasies will look.

In all, more than 200 recipes were selected, developed and tested in the Betty Crocker Kitchens to translate the almost universal appeal of chocolate into a cookbook for chocolate fanciers everywhere.

Betty Crocker

Editors, Lois Tlusty, Terri Berkness; Recipe Development Editor, Ginny Allen; Copy Editor, Faith Sellman; Copywriter, Elizabeth Lemmer; Food Styling Coordinator, Cindy Lund; Food Stylists, Carol Grones, Maria Rolandelli; Art Directors, John Currie, Guy Bowen; Prop Styling, Gail Bailey, Mary O'Brien; Photographer, Steven Smith

PRENTICE HALL PRESS
15 Columbus Circle
New York, NY 10023

Copyright © 1985 by General Mills, Inc., Minneapolis, Minnesota

All rights reserved, including the right of
reproduction in whole or in part in any form.

PRENTICE HALL PRESS and colophons are registered trademarks
of Simon & Schuster, Inc.

BETTY CROCKER is a registered trademark
of General Mills, Inc.

Library of Congress Cataloging-in-Publication Data

Crocker, Betty. [Chocolate cookbook]
Betty Crocker's chocolate cookbook.
p.   cm.
Reprint. Originally published: New York : Random House, 1985.
Includes index.
ISBN 0-13-084997-9
1. Cookery (Chocolate)   I. Title.   II. Title: Chocolate cookbook.   [TX767.C5C76   1991]
641.6'374—dc20   90-39875
                                                                                                                         CIP

Manufactured in the United States of America
10 9 8 7 6 5 4 3 2 1
First Prentice Hall Press Edition

Contents

Pictured on Page 2:

1. Easy Walnut Torte, 2. Apricot and Pudding Parfait, 3. Pinwheels, 4. Classic French Silk Pie, 5. Sour Cream Chocolate Cake, 6. Frosted Brownies, 7. Truffles, 8. Chocolate Chip Cookies, 9. Chocolate Mousse

Know Your Chocolate

The History of Chocolate

The first cocoa tree grew in either Central or South America. However, it was in Mexico where hot chocolate was tasted for the first time — by the Spanish explorer, Hernando Cortez in 1519. It was the royal drink and Emperor Montezuma served the very bitter "chocolatl" to his Spanish guests. The Spaniards were more creative by adding cane sugar to sweeten it and make a more pleasant drink. Others added cinnamon or vanilla and some decided the drink tasted better served hot.

The Spaniards succeeded in keeping cocoa a secret for nearly 100 years but the Spanish monks finally let the secret out. The acceptance of the chocolate drink quickly spread across Europe and in 1657 the first of the famous English Chocolate Houses opened in England. The first chocolate factory was established in the United States in New England in 1765.

The history of chocolate was marked by three revolutionary developments in the 1800's. The invention of the 1828 cocoa press helped to improve the quality of chocolate by squeezing out part of the cocoa butter which made drinking chocolate smoother and more pleasant tasting. In 1876, in Switzerland, Daniel Peter invented a way of making milk chocolate for eating. The third development was a smooth fondant chocolate that replaced the coarse grained chocolate on the market.

The many varieties of cocoa trees grow in the moist, tropical countries near the equator. The seeds or "cocoa beans" in the pods are the source of all chocolate and cocoa. After the pods are picked, they are broken open and the 20 to 50 cocoa beans removed. The beans themselves don't have the chocolate color or fragrance that we are familiar with.

The beans then go through a fermenting process that helps produce chocolate flavor during roasting. After drying, the beans are roasted and the husk removed from the meat or "nibs." The nibs contain an average of 53% cocoa butter and are the bases for chocolate and cocoa products. When the nibs are ground, the cocoa butter is liquified and is turned into a rich brown liquid known as "chocolate liquid" or "chocolate liquor."

The procedure for making chocolate and cocoa are the same until chocolate liquid is formed. Unsweetened chocolate, also known as bitter, cooking or baking chocolate, is the chocolate liquid that has been poured into molds, cooled and hardened. Most of the cocoa butter is removed to make cocoa and cocoa butter is added to make eating chocolate such as candy bars, sweet and milk chocolate.

To make cocoa the cocoa butter is squeezed from the chocolate liquid and drained off.

The remaining hard brown cake is pulverized, sometimes mixed with additional ingredients, and sifted and packaged as cocoa.

Combining melted chocolate liquid with cocoa butter, sugar and flavorings is the beginning of eating chocolate. Milk or cream is added at this stage to make milk chocolate. The mixture is ground and kneaded to develop a smooth texture and pleasant chocolate flavor. The mixture is tempered before it is poured into molds of various sizes and shapes.

Chocolate and Cocoa Terms

CHOCOLATE-FLAVORED:

This term is used for food products flavored with cocoa and/or chocolate liquor, but not containing enough of these substances to be called chocolate as defined by the Standards of Identity (see below).

STANDARDS OF IDENTITY:

A set of standards established by the Food and Drug Administration, which designates for chocolate and cocoa products the percentage of ingredients that must be present in order for them to bear the name of that product.

A. PREMELTED UNSWEETENED CHOCOLATE:

A mixture of cocoa and vegetable oil in 1-ounce foil or plastic envelopes. It is a convenience product that can be used in place of melted unsweetened chocolate.

B. HOT COCOA MIX:

A blend of cocoa, sugar, milk solids and other flavorings used to make a beverage by adding hot water.

C. UNSWEETENED CHOCOLATE:

(Sometimes referred to as bitter, baking or cooking chocolate.) Chocolate liquor which has been cooled and molded, usually in blocks.

D. CHOCOLATE-FLAVORED SYRUP:

Commonly referred to as chocolate syrup. A mixture, in varying proportions, of cocoa or chocolate liquor, sugar, water, salt and sometimes other flavorings such as vanilla.

E. POWDERED CHOCOLATE FLAVORING FOR MILK:

A blend of cocoa, sugar and other flavorings used to make hot and cold beverages by adding milk.

F. MILK CHOCOLATE:

A combination of chocolate liquor, added cocoa butter, sugar, milk or cream. It must contain at least 10% chocolate liquor. It is commonly available in candy bars as well as other forms of candy and chocolate chips.

G. SWEET (DARK) CHOCOLATE:

A combination of chocolate liquor, additional cocoa butter, and sugar. It must contain at least 15% chocolate liquor, and has a higher proportion of sugar than semi-sweet chocolate. One well known form is German sweet cooking chocolate.

H. COCOA BUTTER:

A unique vegetable fat extracted from chocolate liquor by "pressing" at high pressure.

I. CHOCOLATE FUDGE TOPPING:

Similar to chocolate flavored syrup, but with the addition of milk, cream or butter.

J. CACAO (COCOA) BEANS:

The source of chocolate and cocoa, cacao beans are the fruit of the cacao tree, which grows mainly in Latin America and West Africa.

K. NIBS:

The "meat" of the cacao bean. After the beans are cleaned and roasted at controlled temperatures to bring out the full flavor and aroma, the outer shells are removed, leaving the nibs.

L. COMPOUND CHOCOLATE:

A term used for products in which most or all of the cocoa butter has been removed and replaced by another vegetable fat. It can be purchased as white chocolate, vanilla-flavored candy coating, white, confectioners' or summer coating or pastel coating. It is available in dark, white or pastel colors.

M. SEMISWEET CHOCOLATE:

A combination of chocolate liquor, additional cocoa butter and sugar. It must contain at least 35% chocolate liquor. Usually in the form of semi-sweet chocolate chips or squares.

N. COCOA POWDER:

The dry substance of chocolate liquor that remains after most of the cocoa butter has been extracted. Dutch Process cocoa is darker, and the flavor slightly different, from that of natural cocoa.

Storing Chocolate

To maintain its quality, chocolate must be stored properly. It is important to store it in a dry, cool place, between 60° and 78°F. If the temperature is higher than 78° or the humidity is above 50%, chocolate should be kept in a moisture-tight container or wrapped in moistureproof wrap. Chocolate can be stored in the refrigerator if tightly wrapped to keep out moisture and odors. When cold, chocolate becomes hard and brittle so remove it from the refrigerator and let stand at room temperature before using.

When chocolate is stored at temperatures warmer than 78°, the cocoa butter will melt and rise to the surface, causing a grayish-white film called "bloom." Bloom does not affect the quality and flavor of the chocolate, only the appearance. When the chocolate is melted or used in cooking, it will regain its original rich, brown color.

Cocoa is less sensitive to temperature and humidity changes because the cocoa butter has been removed. However, it is best to store cocoa in a tightly covered container in a dry, cool place. When stored at a high temperature or high humidity, it may become lumpy and lose some of its rich brown color.

Melting Chocolate

There are two important rules to follow when melting chocolate:

1. Be sure all equipment used for melting chocolate is dry. It is the very small amount of moisture, such as a drop of water or even steam that causes chocolate to "tighten" or become thick and sometimes grainy.

2. Chocolate scorches easily, therefore it should never be melted over high heat.

Methods for melting chocolate include:

Direct heat: Place chocolate in heavy saucepan. Heat over low heat, stirring constantly, just until chocolate is melted. Remove pan from heat; stir chocolate until smooth. If squares or large chunks of chocolate are to be melted, chop the chocolate into smaller pieces for faster and more even melting.

Double boiler: Place water in bottom pan of double boiler so that it comes to within ½ inch of top pan. Heat water to boiling, then reduce heat. Place chocolate in the top pan; place over the hot water. Keep over low heat, stirring occasionally, until chocolate is melted (the water should be simmering, not boiling).

Microwave: Place chocolate in a microwavable container. Microwave uncovered on medium (50%), stirring once every minute, just until chocolate is melted. Stir chocolate until smooth. It is important to stir chocolate frequently when melting as some chocolate retains its shape when softened.

Water bath: Place the chocolate in a custard cup, small saucepan or small heatproof bowl. Place the container with the chocolate in a pan of hot, not boiling, water over very low heat. The water should not be boiling because the steam could cause the chocolate to "tighten." Heat, stirring constantly, just until the chocolate is melted. Remove container from the water; stir the chocolate until smooth.

Questions and Answers

What causes chocolate to become thick and lumpy during melting?

A very small amount of moisture can cause chocolate to become thick, lumpy and sometimes grainy during melting. This is often referred to as "tightening." Be sure all utensils are completely dry and that no steam, if using a water bath or double boiler for melting, gets into the chocolate.

Can chocolate that has been tightened be used?

Yes, if moisture should accidentally get into the chocolate, this can be corrected. Stir in 1 teaspoon vegetable oil or shortening for every 1 ounce of chocolate. Do not use margarine or butter because they contain a small amount of water.

Can the type of chocolate be substituted in a recipe?

For best results, use the type of chocolate called for in the recipe. Do not substitute semisweet or milk chocolate for unsweetened chocolate.

When can premelted chocolate be used as a substitute?

Premelted chocolate can be substituted in a recipe calling for unsweetened chocolate or cocoa. A one-ounce envelope equals ¼ cup cocoa or a 1 ounce square of unsweetened chocolate.

What causes milk chocolate to stiffen when melted?

High temperature causes milk chocolate to stiffen so it is best to melt it in a water bath or a double boiler over hot, not boiling, water.

What is the grayish-white film that sometimes forms on chocolate?

Chocolate has a high content of cocoa butter. When chocolate is stored at temperatures that vary from hot to cold, it can develop a grayish-white film, caused by the cocoa butter melting and rising to the surface, which is referred to as "bloom." This bloom does not affect the quality or taste of the chocolate and the chocolate will regain its rich color when melted.

How do you measure cocoa?

Lightly spoon cocoa into a dry measuring cup and level off the top with a spatula.

How do you combine melted chocolate and beaten egg whites?

Chocolate deflates stiffly beaten egg whites so fold the chocolate mixture into egg whites carefully and just until blended.

How do you store chocolate-flavored syrup?

After the syrup is opened, it should be covered and stored in the refrigerator. Shake the can of chocolate-flavored syrup before you open it so it is an even consistency. If the syrup becomes too thick, place can in lukewarm water until syrup is of pouring consistency.

What is "white chocolate"?

By true definition, white chocolate is not chocolate because it does not contain any chocolate liquor, which gives chocolate its flavor. However, because it has similar texture and some common ingredients to milk chocolate, it is often referred to as "chocolate." It is also known as white candy coating, vanilla-flavored candy coating, pastel coating, confectioners' coating or compound chocolate. It is made from a combination of sugar, vegetable shortening, milk solids, flavorings and sometimes color is added. Sometimes the fat can be cocoa butter rather than vegetable shortening.

Does chocolate contain caffeine?

Yes, chocolate does contain caffeine and therefore is classified as a stimulant.

What is carob and can it be substituted in recipe calling for chocolate?

Carob powder is made from the dried pods of the carob tree. When ground and roasted, carob has a similar taste and appearance to cocoa. Carob can be substituted in recipes calling for cocoa but you may want to use more carob than cocoa for the necessary flavor level. Carob does not contain caffeine.

Chocolate Substitutions

When recipe calls for:	You can use:
1 square (1 ounce) unsweetened chocolate, melted	1 envelope (1 ounce) premelted chocolate OR 3 tablespoons unsweetened cocoa plus 1 tablespoon vegetable shortening or oil
3 squares (1 ounce each) semisweet chocolate	½ cup (3 ounces) semisweet chocolate chips

Cakes & Pies

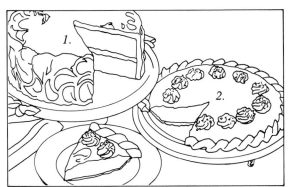

1. Sour Cream Chocolate Cake, 2. Chocolate Chiffon Pie

Sour Cream Chocolate Cake

2   cups all-purpose flour
2   cups sugar
1   cup water
3/4 cup dairy sour cream
1/4 cup shortening
1 1/4 teaspoons baking soda
1   teaspoon salt
1   teaspoon vanilla
1/2 teaspoon baking powder
2   eggs
4   squares (1 ounce each) unsweetened
    chocolate, melted and cooled
    Sour Cream Chocolate Frosting or
    Fudge Frosting (right)

Heat oven to 350°. Grease and flour rectangular pan, 13 × 9 × 2 inches, or 2 round pans, 9 × 1½ inches or 3 round pans, 8 × 1½ inches. Beat all ingredients except frosting on low speed, scraping bowl constantly, 30 seconds. Beat on high speed, scraping bowl occasionally, 3 minutes. Pour into pan(s).

Bake until wooden pick inserted in center comes out clean, rectangle 40 to 45 minutes, layers 30 to 35 minutes; cool. Frost rectangle or fill and frost layers with Sour Cream Chocolate Frosting.

Sour Cream Chocolate Frosting

1/3 cup margarine or butter, softened
3   squares (1 ounce each) unsweetened
    chocolate, melted and cooled
3   cups powdered sugar
1/2 cup dairy sour cream
2   teaspoons vanilla

Mix margarine and chocolate; stir in sugar. Stir in sour cream and vanilla; beat until frosting is smooth and of spreading consistency.

Fudge Frosting

2   cups sugar
1/2 cup shortening
2/3 cup milk
1/2 teaspoon salt
3   squares (1 ounce each) unsweetened
    chocolate or 3 envelopes (1 ounce each)
    premelted chocolate
2   teaspoons vanilla

Mix all ingredients except vanilla in 2½-quart saucepan. Heat to rolling boil, stirring occasionally. Boil 1 minute without stirring. Place pan in bowl of ice and water. Beat until frosting is of spreading consistency; stir in vanilla.

SOUR CREAM CHOCOLATE CUPCAKES: Pour batter into paper-lined medium muffin cups, 2½ × 1¼ inches, filling each about ½ full. Bake until wooden pick inserted in center comes out clean, 20 to 25 minutes. About 3 dozen cupcakes.

YIELDS FOR CAKES	
Size and Kind	Servings
8-inch layer cake	10 to 14
9-inch layer cake	12 to 16
13 × 9 × 2-inch rectangular cake	12 to 15
8- or 9-inch square cake	9
angel or chiffon cake	12 to 16

Dark Chocolate Cake

2 cups all-purpose flour
2 cups sugar
½ cup shortening
¾ cup water
¾ cup buttermilk
1 teaspoon baking soda
1 teaspoon salt
1 teaspoon vanilla
½ teaspoon baking powder
2 eggs
4 squares (1 ounce each) unsweetened
   chocolate, melted and cooled
   White Mountain Frosting (below)

Heat oven to 350°. Grease and flour 2 round pans, 9 × 1½ inches, rectangular pan, 13 × 9 × 2 inches, or 12-cup bundt cake pan. Beat all ingredients except frosting on low speed, scraping bowl constantly, 30 seconds. Beat on high speed, scraping bowl occasionally, 3 minutes. Pour into pan(s).

Bake until wooden pick inserted in center comes out clean, layers 30 to 35 minutes, rectangle 40 to 45 minutes, bundt cake 50 to 55 minutes. Cool layers or bundt cake 10 minutes; remove from pan(s). Frost rectangle or fill and frost layers with White Mountain Frosting. Sprinkle bundt cake with powdered sugar or drizzle with Chocolate Glaze (page 20)

White Mountain Frosting

½ cup sugar
¼ cup light or dark corn syrup
2 tablespoons water
2 egg whites (¼ cup)
1 teaspoon vanilla

Mix sugar, corn syrup and water in small saucepan. Cover; heat to rolling boil over medium heat. Uncover; boil rapidly to 242° on candy thermometer or until small amount of mixture dropped into very cold water forms a firm ball that holds its shape until pressed. As mixture boils, beat egg whites until stiff peaks form. Pour hot syrup very slowly in a thin stream into egg whites, beating constantly on medium speed. Beat on high speed until stiff peaks form. Stir in vanilla during last minute of beating.

COCOA FROSTING: Sift ¼ cup cocoa over frosting and gently fold in until blended.

CHERRY-NUT FROSTING: Stir in ¼ cup cut-up candied cherries and ¼ cup chopped nuts.

PINK MOUNTAIN FROSTING: Substitute 2 tablespoons maraschino cherry syrup for the water.

PEPPERMINT FROSTING: Stir in ⅓ cup coarsely crushed peppermint candy (1 stick) or ½ teaspoon peppermint extract.

CHOCOLATE REVEL FROSTING: Stir in ½ cup miniature semisweet chocolate chips or 1 square (1 ounce) coarsely grated semisweet or unsweetened chocolate.

SATINY BEIGE FROSTING: Substitute ½ cup packed brown sugar for the ½ cup granulated sugar and decrease vanilla to ½ teaspoon.

Chocolate Wedges

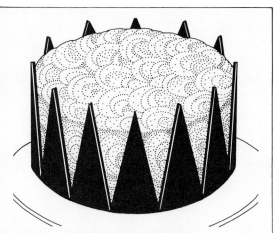

Heat 2 bars (4 ounces each) sweet cooking chocolate, cut up, over low heat, stirring frequently, until melted. Spread over outside bottom of 8- or 9-inch round layer pan (use same size as for cake). Refrigerate until firm; bring to room temperature. Cut into 12 to 16 wedges. Refrigerate until ready to place on frosted cake. Arrange wedges upright in frosting around side of cake. To serve, cut between wedges.

Buttermallow Cake

1³/₄ cups all-purpose flour
 1 cup granulated sugar
 ¹/₂ cup packed brown sugar
1¹/₂ teaspoons baking soda
 ³/₄ teaspoon salt
 ¹/₂ cup shortening
1¹/₄ cups buttermilk
 2 eggs
 2 squares (1 ounce each) unsweetened
    chocolate or 1 bar (4 ounces) sweet cooking
    chocolate, melted and cooled
 1 teaspoon vanilla
 ¹/₂ teaspoon red food color
    Butterscotch Filling (below)
 ¹/₂ cup chopped nuts
    Marshmallow Frosting (right)

Heat oven to 350°. Grease and flour rectangular pan, 13 × 9 × 2 inches. Beat all ingredients except filling, nuts and frosting on low speed, scraping bowl constantly, 30 seconds. Beat on high speed, scraping bowl occasionally, 3 minutes. Pour into pan.

Bake until wooden pick inserted in center comes out clean, 35 to 40 minutes; cool 10 minutes. Remove from pan if desired and cool completely.

Prepare Filling; spread over top of cake to within ¹/₂ inch of edges. Sprinkle nuts over filling. Frost sides and top of cake with Marshmallow Frosting.

Butterscotch Filling

¹/₂ cup packed brown sugar
¹/₄ cup cornstarch
¹/₄ teaspoon salt
¹/₂ cup water
 1 tablespoon margarine or butter

Stir together sugar, cornstarch, salt and water in saucepan. Cook over low heat, stirring con-stantly, until mixture thickens and boils. Boil and stir 1 minute. Blend in margarine; cool.

Marshmallow Frosting

 2 egg whites
1¹/₂ cups sugar
 ¹/₄ teaspoon cream of tartar
 ¹/₃ cup water
 1 tablespoon light corn syrup
 ³/₄ cup marshmallow crème or 16 (about ¹/₄
    pound) marshmallows, quartered

In top of double boiler, combine egg whites, sugar, cream of tartar, water and syrup. Place over boiling water; beat on high speed until stiff peaks form, about 7 minutes. Remove pan from heat. Beat in marshmallow crème until frosting is of spreading consistency.

RED DEVILS FOOD LAYER CAKE: Pour batter into 3 greased and floured round pans, 8 × 1¹/₂ inches, or 2 round pans, 9 × 1¹/₂ inches. Bake until wooden pick inserted in center comes out clean, 30 to 35 minutes. Let stand 10 minutes; remove from pans. Cool completely. Fill and frost side and top with French Silk Frosting (below) or Brown Sugar Frosting (page 18). Press chopped nuts into side of cake if desired.

French Silk Frosting

2²/₃ cups powdered sugar
 ²/₃ cup margarine or butter, softened
 2 squares (1 ounce each) unsweetened
    chocolate or 1 bar (4 ounces) sweet cooking
    chocolate, melted and cooled
 ³/₄ teaspoon vanilla
 2 tablespoons milk

Beat sugar, margarine, chocolate and vanilla in 1¹/₂-quart bowl, scraping bowl frequently, on low speed. Gradually beat in milk until smooth and of spreading consistency.

Red Devils Food Layer Cake

Black Midnight Cake

2¼ cups all-purpose flour
1⅔ cups sugar
⅔ cup cocoa
¾ cup shortening
1¼ cups water
1¼ teaspoons baking soda
1 teaspoon salt
¼ teaspoon baking powder
1 teaspoon vanilla
2 eggs
Brown Sugar Chocolate Frosting (below)

Heat oven to 350°. Grease and flour rectangular pan, 13 × 9 × 2 inches, or 2 round pans, 9 × 1½ inches or 3 round pans, 8 × 1½ inches. Beat all ingredients except frosting on low speed, scraping bowl constantly, 30 seconds. Beat on high speed, scraping bowl occasionally, 3 minutes. Pour into pan(s).

Bake until wooden pick inserted in center comes out clean, rectangle 40 to 45 minutes, layers 30 to 35 minutes; cool. Frost rectangle or fill and frost layers with Brown Sugar Chocolate Frosting.

Brown Sugar Chocolate Frosting

2 cups packed brown sugar
¼ cup plus 2 tablespoons cocoa
½ cup shortening
½ cup milk
3 cups powdered sugar
2 teaspoons vanilla

Mix brown sugar, cocoa, shortening and milk in saucepan. Cook, stirring frequently, until mixture begins to boil around the edges (200°). Remove from heat and cool to lukewarm (110°). Add powdered sugar and vanilla; beat until smooth and creamy and of spreading consistency. If frosting thickens too much to spread, stir in additional milk.

BROWN SUGAR FROSTING: Omit Cocoa.

Chocolate Sundae Cake

2⅓ cups all-purpose flour
1½ cups sugar
½ cup shortening
¾ cup buttermilk
½ cup water
½ cup chocolate-flavored syrup
1 teaspoon baking soda
1 teaspoon salt
½ teaspoon baking powder
1 teaspoon vanilla
2 eggs
½ cup chocolate-flavored syrup
Chocolate Sundae Frosting (below)
1 to 2 tablespoons chocolate-flavored syrup

Heat oven to 350°. Grease and flour rectangular pan, 13 × 9 × 2 inches, 12-cup bundt cake pan, 2 round pans, 9 × 1½ inches, or 3 round pans, 8 × 1½ inches. Beat all ingredients except ½ cup chocolate-flavored syrup, the frosting and 1 tablespoon chocolate-flavored syrup on low speed, scraping bowl constantly, 30 seconds. Beat on medium speed, scraping bowl occasionally, 3 minutes.

Reserving ½ cup of the batter, pour into pan(s). Mix remaining ½ cup syrup into reserved batter. Pour half of the mixture over batter in each pan. Cut through batter several times for marbled effect.

Bake until wooden pick inserted in center comes out clean, rectangle about 40 minutes, bundt cake 50 to 55 minutes, 9-inch layers about 35 minutes, 8-inch layers about 25 minutes. Cool layers or bundt cake 10 minutes; remove from pan(s). Cool completely. Frost rectangle or fill and frost layers with Chocolate Sundae Frosting and drizzle 1 to 2 tablespoons chocolate-flavored syrup over top. Or top slices of bundt cake with Chocolate Sundae Frosting. Refrigerate any remaining cake.

Chocolate Sundae Frosting

Beat 1 cup chilled whipping cream and ¼ cup chocolate syrup in chilled bowl until stiff.

Cherry-Chocolate Cake

2 cups all-purpose flour
2 cups sugar
1 teaspoon baking soda
1 teaspoon salt
½ teaspoon baking powder
¾ cup water
¾ cup buttermilk
½ cup shortening
2 eggs
1 teaspoon vanilla
4 squares (1 ounce each) unsweetened
    chocolate, melted and cooled
20 maraschino cherries, finely cut up and
    drained
½ teaspoon almond extract
    Cherry-Chocolate Frosting (below)

Heat oven to 350°. Grease and flour rectangular pan, 13 × 9 × 2 inches, or 3 round pans, 8 × 1½ inches or 2 round pans, 9 × 1½ inches. Beat all ingredients except frosting on low speed, scraping bowl constantly, 30 seconds. Beat on high speed, scraping bowl occasionally, 3 minutes. Pour batter into pan(s).

Bake until wooden pick inserted in center comes out clean, rectangle 40 to 45 minutes, layers 30 to 35 minutes; cool. Frost rectangle or fill and frost layers with Cherry-Chocolate Frosting.

Cherry-Chocolate Frosting

¼ cup margarine or butter, softened
2 squares (1 ounce each) unsweetened
    chocolate, melted and cooled
2 cups powdered sugar
¼ teaspoon almond extract
3 to 4 tablespoons maraschino cherry
    syrup

Mix margarine, chocolate and sugar. Stir in extract and cherry syrup; beat until smooth and of spreading consistency.

Easy Chocolate Patterns

Frost cake with any fluffy white frosting. Melt 1 square (1 ounce) unsweetened chocolate as directed on page 10 or use chocolate-flavored syrup. Cool melted chocolate slightly. Using a teaspoon, drizzle the chocolate over the frosted cake in one of the following ways.

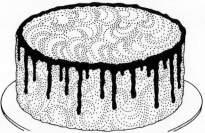

Allegretti: Drizzle melted chocolate around top edge of cake, letting it run down side unevenly.

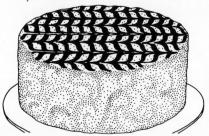

Feather Pattern: Drizzle several parallel lines of melted chocolate across top of cake. Immediately draw a spatula or knife back and forth across lines. Or for a different effect draw spatula across lines in the same direction each time.

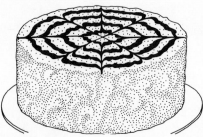

Geometric Pattern: Pour melted chocolate in circles on frosted layer cake beginning with small circle in center and encircling with larger circles 1 inch apart. Draw a spatula or knife from center outward and from outside inward alternately 8 times. Or for a different effect draw the spatula from center outward each time.

Coconut-Orange Cake

2 cups all-purpose flour
2 cups sugar
1/2 cup shortening
3/4 cup water
3/4 cup buttermilk
2 teaspoons ground cinnamon
1 teaspoon baking soda
1 teaspoon salt
1/2 teaspoon baking powder
1/2 teaspoon ground nutmeg
2 eggs
4 squares (1 ounce each) unsweetened
   chocolate, melted and cooled
1 1/2 cups flaked coconut
1/2 cup orange marmalade
   Chocolate Glaze (right)
   Orange-Cheese Frosting (right)
1 cup flaked coconut

Heat oven to 350°. Grease and flour 2 round pans, 9 × 1 1/2 inches, or 3 round pans, 8 × 1 1/2 inches. Beat flour, sugar, shortening, water, buttermilk, cinnamon, baking soda, salt, baking powder, nutmeg, eggs and chocolate on medium speed, scraping bowl constantly, until blended, about 30 seconds. Beat on high speed, scraping bowl occasionally, 3 minutes. Stir in 1 1/2 cups coconut. Pour into pans.

Bake until wooden pick inserted in center comes out clean, 30 to 35 minutes; cool 10 minutes. Remove from pans; cool cake completely.

Fill layers with orange marmalade. Prepare Chocolate Glaze; spread evenly over top of cake. Prepare Orange-Cheese Frosting; reserve 1 cup. Frost side of cake with remaining frosting. Press 1 cup coconut around side of cake. Place reserved frosting in decorating bag with large open star tip #4B. Pipe large rosettes around top edge of cake. Garnish with pared orange sections if desired. Refrigerate any remaining cake.

Chocolate Glaze

Heat 3 squares (1 ounce each) semisweet chocolate, 1 tablespoon margarine or butter and 1 tablespoon corn syrup over low heat, stirring constantly, until chocolate is melted; cool slightly.

Orange-Cheese Frosting

1 cup chilled whipping cream
1 package (3 ounces) cream cheese, softened
1 cup powdered sugar
1 teaspoon grated orange peel

Beat whipping cream in chilled 1 1/2-quart bowl until stiff. Mix cream cheese, powdered sugar and orange peel. Fold cream cheese mixture into whipped cream.

WRITING WITH CHOCOLATE

Heat 1/3 cup semisweet chocolate chips in saucepan over low heat, stirring occasionally, until melted, or prepare one of the decorator frostings below. Place the melted chocolate or decorator frosting in a decorating bag with small writing tip or in small sturdy plastic bag. Cut off small corner of plastic bag, about 1/8-inch diameter. Write desired message (birthday, congratulations, etc.) on frosted cake or cupcakes.

Cocoa Decorator Frosting: Mix 1/2 cup powdered sugar, 2 teaspoons cocoa and 1 1/2 teaspoons water until smooth and desired consistency. Add water if necessary.

Chocolate Decorator Frosting: Heat 1 square (1 ounce) unsweetened chocolate and 1 teaspoon shortening over low heat until chocolate is melted. Remove from heat. Stir in 1 to 2 tablespoons powdered sugar, 1 teaspoon at a time, until smooth and desired consistency.

Irish Coffee Chocolate Cake

Irish Coffee Chocolate Cake

2¼ cups all-purpose flour
1½ cups sugar
2¼ teaspoons baking powder
½ teaspoon salt
1⅔ cups chilled whipping cream
3 eggs
1 teaspoon vanilla
3 squares (1 ounce each) unsweetened
    chocolate, melted and cooled
3 tablespoons instant coffee
2 tablespoons sugar
½ cup Irish whiskey or other whiskey
    Irish Coffee Frosting (right)
1 package (6 ounces) semisweet chocolate
    chips

Heat oven to 350°. Grease and flour 2 round pans, 8 or 9 × 1½ inches. Mix flour, 1½ cups sugar, the baking powder and salt. Beat whipping cream in chilled 3-quart bowl until stiff. Beat eggs until thick and lemon colored, about 5 minutes. Fold eggs, vanilla and chocolate into whipped cream. Add flour mixture, about ½ cup at a time, folding gently after each addition, until blended. Pour into pans.

Bake until wooden pick inserted in center comes out clean, 8-inch layers 35 to 40 minutes, 9-inch layers 30 to 35 minutes; cool 10 minutes. Remove from pans; cool cake completely. Mix coffee (dry), 2 tablespoons sugar and the whiskey; stir until coffee is dissolved.

Place cake layers on wire racks over waxed paper. Poke holes in top of cake with skewer or long-tined fork. Pour half of the coffee mixture evenly over each layer; let stand at room temperature at least 30 minutes.

Reserve ½ cup Irish Coffee Frosting for decorating if desired; fill layers and frost side and top of cake with remaining frosting. Heat chocolate chips over low heat, stirring constantly, until melted; cool slightly. Place chocolate in small sturdy plastic bag or in decorating bag with medium writing tip. Cut off small corner of plastic bag, about ¼-inch diameter. Pipe chocolate in lattice design across top of cake. Place reserved frosting in decorating bag with open star tip #32 or 4B. Pipe shell border or rosettes around top edge of cake.

Irish Coffee Frosting

1 tablespoon instant coffee
2 tablespoons Irish whiskey or other
    whiskey
2⅔ cups powdered sugar
⅔ cup margarine or butter, softened
1 teaspoon vanilla

Stir coffee (dry) into whiskey until coffee is dissolved. Beat coffee mixture, powdered sugar, margarine and vanilla on medium speed until smooth.

German Chocolate Cake

This is the grass roots recipe that swept the country to become a classic.

½ cup boiling water
1 bar (4 ounces) sweet cooking chocolate
2 cups sugar
1 cup margarine or butter, softened
4 egg yolks
1 teaspoon vanilla
2½ cups cake flour
1 teaspoon baking soda
1 teaspoon salt
1 cup buttermilk
4 egg whites, stiffly beaten
Coconut-Pecan Frosting (below)

Heat oven to 350°. Grease 3 round pans, 8 or 9 × 1½ inches, or 2 square pans, 8 × 8 × 2 or 9 × 9 × 2 inches. Line bottoms of pans with waxed paper. Pour boiling water over chocolate in small bowl, stirring until chocolate is melted; set aside to cool.

Beat sugar and margarine in 2½-quart bowl until light and fluffy. Beat in egg yolks, one at a time. Beat in chocolate and vanilla on low speed. Mix in flour, baking soda and salt alternately with buttermilk, beating after each addition until batter is smooth. Fold in egg whites. Divide batter among pans.

Bake until wooden pick inserted in center comes out clean, 8-inch rounds 35 to 40 minutes, 9-inch rounds 30 to 35 minutes, 8-inch squares 45 to 50 minutes, 9-inch squares 40 to 45 minutes; cool. Fill layers and frost top of cake with Coconut-Pecan Frosting.

Coconut-Pecan Frosting

1 cup sugar
1 cup evaporated milk
½ cup margarine or butter
3 egg yolks
1 teaspoon vanilla
1⅓ cups flaked coconut
1 cup chopped pecans

Mix sugar, evaporated milk, margarine, egg yolks and vanilla in 1-quart saucepan. Cook over medium heat, stirring occasionally, until thick, about 12 minutes. Stir in coconut and pecans. Beat until of spreading consistency.

Peanut Cake

2¼ cups all-purpose flour
1¾ cups sugar
½ cup shortening
1½ cups buttermilk
1½ teaspoons baking soda
1 teaspoon salt
2 teaspoons vanilla
2 eggs
2 squares (1 ounce each) unsweetened chocolate, melted and cooled
½ cup finely chopped salted peanuts
Sour Cream Frosting (below)
About ¼ cup crushed peanut brittle

Heat oven to 350°. Grease and flour 2 round pans, 9 × 1½ inches. Beat all ingredients except frosting and peanut brittle on low speed, scraping bowl constantly, 30 seconds. Beat on medium speed, scraping bowl frequently, 2 minutes. Pour into pans.

Bake until wooden pick inserted in center comes out clean, 30 to 35 minutes. Cool 10 minutes; remove from pans. Fill and frost cake with Sour Cream Frosting. Decorate with peanut brittle.

Sour Cream Frosting

2½ cups powdered sugar
¾ cup all-purpose flour
⅓ cup margarine or butter, softened
⅓ cup dairy sour cream
2 teaspoons vanilla
½ teaspoon salt

Mix all ingredients until smooth. If necessary, stir in 1 to 2 tablespoons additional sour cream until smooth and of spreading consistency.

Nesselrode Cake

2 cups all-purpose flour
2 cups sugar
½ cup shortening
¾ cup water
¾ cup buttermilk
1 teaspoon baking soda
1 teaspoon salt
1 teaspoon vanilla
½ teaspoon baking powder
2 eggs
4 squares (1 ounce each) unsweetened
  chocolate, melted and cooled
  Nesselrode Filling (below)
  Cocoa Fluff (below)

Heat oven to 350°. Grease and flour 3 round pans, 8 × 1½ inches. Beat all ingredients except Nesselrode Filling and Cocoa Fluff on low speed, scraping bowl constantly, 30 seconds. Beat on medium speed, scraping bowl occasionally, 3 minutes. Pour into pans.

Bake until wooden pick inserted in center comes out clean, 30 to 35 minutes; cool. Fill layers and frost top of cake with Nesselrode Filling. Frost side of cake with Cococa Fluff. Refrigerate any remaining cake.

Nesselrode Filling

Beat 1 cup chilled whipping cream and ¼ cup powdered sugar in chilled 1½-quart bowl until stiff. Fold in ¼ cup Nesselrode* and about 6 drops red food color.

Cocoa Fluff

Beat 1 cup chilled whipping cream, ¼ cup powdered sugar and 2 tablespoons cocoa in chilled 1½-quart bowl until stiff.

*¼ cup finely cut-up candied fruit and 1 teaspoon rum flavoring can be substituted for the Nesselrode.

NOTE: Cake can be baked in 2 round pans, 9 × 1½ inches. When cool, split to make 4 layers. Divide Nesselrode Filling into 4 parts. Fill layers and frost top of cake.

Honey Chocolate Cake

1¾ cups all-purpose flour
¾ cup sugar
½ cup shortening
¾ cup buttermilk
½ cup honey
1 teaspoon baking soda
½ teaspoon salt
2 eggs
2 squares (1 ounce each) unsweetened
  chocolate, melted and cooled
  Honey Butter Frosting (below)

Heat oven to 350°. Grease and flour 2 round pans, 8 or 9 × 1½ inches. Beat all ingredients except frosting on medium speed, scraping bowl constantly, until blended, about 30 seconds. Beat on high speed, scraping bowl occasionally, 3 minutes. Pour batter into pans.

Bake until wooden pick inserted in center comes out clean, 30 to 35 minutes; cool 10 minutes. Remove from pans; cool completely. Fill and frost cake with Honey Butter Frosting. Garnish with Chocolate-dipped Almonds (below) if desired.

Honey Butter Frosting

Mix 3 cups powdered sugar, ⅓ cup margarine or butter, softened, 3 tablespoons honey and 2 tablespoons milk; beat until frosting is smooth and spreading consistency. If necessary, stir in additional milk, ½ teaspoon at a time.

CHOCOLATE-DIPPED ALMONDS

Heat ¼ cup semisweet chocolate chips and ½ teaspoon shortening over low heat, stirring occasionally, until chocolate is melted. Cool slightly. Dip tips of 20 to 30 whole blanched almonds into chocolate mixture; place on waxed paper. Refrigerate until set. Arrange around top edge of frosted cake.

Hazelnut Chocolate Torte

6 eggs, separated
1 tablespoon finely shredded orange peel
¾ teaspoon ground cinnamon
½ cup granulated sugar
1 teaspoon cream of tartar
½ cup granulated sugar
3 cups very finely ground hazelnuts
½ cup all-purpose flour
  Chocolate Butter Frosting (right)
1 cup chilled whipping cream
½ cup powdered sugar
¼ cup cocoa
2 teaspoons finely shredded orange peel
½ cup chopped hazelnuts

Heat oven to 325°. Grease bottom only of springform pan, 9 × 3 inches. Line bottom with waxed paper; grease generously. Beat egg yolks, 1 tablespoon orange peel and the cinnamon in 1½-quart bowl on high speed until very thick and light colored, about 6 minutes. Gradually beat in ½ cup sugar, 1 tablespoon at a time; reserve. Wash beaters.

Beat egg whites and cream of tartar in 2½-quart bowl on high speed until soft peaks form. Gradually beat in ½ cup sugar, 1 tablespoon at a time. Continue beating until stiff peaks form. Fold egg yolk mixture into meringue. Mix 3 cups ground hazelnuts and the flour. Sprinkle about ⅓ of the hazelnut mixture over meringue; fold in. Repeat with remaining hazelnut mixture. Spread in pan.

Bake until wooden pick inserted in center comes out clean, 55 to 60 minutes; cool on wire rack 15 minutes. Loosen side of cake from pan with metal spatula. Carefully remove side of pan. Invert cake on wire rack; remove bottom of pan. Turn cake right side up. Cool cake completely. Wrap tightly; refrigerate at least 4 hours for easier slicing.

Prepare Chocolate Butter Frosting. Reserve 1 cup for decorating. Beat whipping cream, powdered sugar and cocoa in chilled 1½-quart bowl until stiff. Fold in 2 teaspoons orange peel. Carefully split cake horizontally to make 3 layers. Spread 1 layer with half of the whipped cream mixture; repeat. Top with remaining layer. Frost side and top of torte with Chocolate Butter Frosting. Press ½ cup chopped hazelnuts around side.

Place reserved 1 cup Chocolate Butter Frosting in decorating bag with large open star tip #4B. Pipe large rosettes on top of cake. Garnish with whole hazelnuts if desired. Refrigerate at least 8 hours. To cut, use sharp, straight-edge knife. Refrigerate any remaining torte.

Chocolate Butter Frosting

½ cup margarine or butter, softened
3 squares (1 ounce each) unsweetened
  chocolate, melted and cooled or ½ cup cocoa
3 cups powdered sugar
1 tablespoon brandy, if desired
2 teaspoons vanilla
  About 3 tablespoons milk

Beat margarine and chocolate. Beat in remaining ingredients until mixture is smooth and of spreading consistency.

CHOCOLATE FLOWERS

Heat ⅓ cup semisweet chocolate chips in saucepan over low heat, stirring occasionally, until melted. Place chocolate in small sturdy plastic storage bag, parchment cone or decorating bag with small writing tip. If using plastic bag or parchment cone cut off very small tip, about ⅛ inch in diameter. Pipe chocolate in desired design (flowers, butterflies, bows, initials, etc.) onto waxed paper-lined cookie sheet. Refrigerate until set, about 30 minutes. Place as desired on frosted cake, cupcakes or pie.

The design can also be drawn on paper first, if desired, and then placed under the waxed paper to use as a guide. Or the design can be piped directly onto the frosted cake, cupcakes or pie.

Hazlenut Chocolate Torte

Easy Walnut Torte

1½ cups chopped walnuts
1½ cups vanilla wafer crumbs
 1 cup packed brown sugar
 1 cup margarine or butter, melted
 1 package (18.25 ounces) devils food cake
    mix with pudding
1½ cups chilled whipping cream
 3 tablespoons granulated sugar
 1 teaspoon vanilla

Heat oven to 350°. Mix walnuts, wafer crumbs, brown sugar and margarine. Spread about ¾ cup in each of 2 ungreased round pans, 9 × 1½ inches. Prepare cake mix as directed on package. Pour about 1¼ cups batter over walnut mixture in each pan; refrigerate remaining batter.

Bake until top springs back when touched lightly, about 20 minutes. Immediately remove from pans; invert. Repeat with remaining batter and walnut mixture. Cool layers completely.

Beat whipping cream, granulated sugar and vanilla in chilled 1½-quart bowl until stiff. Place 1 layer, walnut side up, on serving plate; spread with whipped cream. Repeat with remaining layers and whipped cream. Frost top of torte with whipped cream. Garnish with Grated Chocolate (below) if desired. Refrigerate.

GRATED CHOCOLATE

Unsweetened, semisweet or sweet chocolate can be used for grating. The chocolate should be cool and firm for grating. Use a hand grater and rub the chocolate across the grating section (size will depend on the use desired). A blender or food processor can also be used but the chocolate should be cut into small pieces first or use chocolate chips. Grated chocolate can be used as a garnish or it can be folded into sweetened whipped cream.

Nut Cracker Sweet Torte

 6 eggs, separated
½ cup sugar
 2 tablespoons vegetable oil
 1 tablespoon rum flavoring
½ cup sugar
¼ cup all-purpose flour
1¼ teaspoons baking powder
 1 teaspoon ground cinnamon
½ teaspoon ground cloves
 1 cup fine graham cracker crumbs (about 12
    squares)
 1 cup finely chopped nuts
 1 square (1 ounce) unsweetened chocolate,
    grated
    Rum-flavored Whipped Cream (below)

Heat oven to 350°. Line bottoms of 2 round pans, 8 or 9 × 1½ inches, with aluminum foil. Beat egg whites in 2½-quart bowl until frothy. Beat in ½ cup sugar, 1 tablespoon at a time; continue beating until stiff. Beat egg yolks, oil and rum flavoring in 1½-quart bowl on low speed until blended. Add ½ cup sugar, the flour, baking powder, cinnamon and cloves; beat on medium speed 1 minute. Fold in crumbs, nuts and chocolate. Pour into pans.

Bake until top springs back when touched lightly, 30 to 35 minutes. Cool 10 minutes. Loosen edges of layers with knife; invert pan and hit sharply on table. (Cake will drop out.) Remove foil; cool completely.

Split cake to make 4 layers. Fill layers and frost top of torte with Rum-flavored Whipped Cream. Garnish with Grated Chocolate (left) or Chocolate Curls (page 27) if desired. Refrigerate torte at least 8 hours but no longer than 24 hours. (Torte mellows and becomes moist with refrigeration.) 12 servings.

Rum-flavored Whipped Cream

Beat 2 cups chilled whipping cream, ½ cup powdered sugar and 2 teaspoons rum flavoring in chilled 1½-quart bowl until stiff.

Sacher Torte

8 squares (1 ounce each) semisweet
   chocolate
1 cup margarine or butter, softened
1 cup powdered sugar
⅔ cup egg yolks (7 or 8), well beaten
⅔ cup fine dry bread crumbs
1 cup egg whites (7 or 8)
⅛ teaspoon salt
1 cup powdered sugar
   Apricot Glaze (below)
   Dark Chocolate Glaze (below)

Heat oven to 350°. Grease and flour 2 round pans, 9 × 1½ inches. Heat chocolate over very low heat, stirring frequently, until melted; cool. Beat margarine and 1 cup powdered sugar in 2½-quart bowl on high speed until light and fluffy. Gradually add egg yolks, beating well after each addition. Beat in cooled chocolate and bread crumbs; reserve.

Beat egg whites and salt in 3-quart bowl until frothy; beat in remaining sugar until soft, round peaks form. Fold chocolate mixture into egg whites. Pour into pans. Bake until wooden pick inserted in center comes out clean, about 40 minutes; cool. Remove cake from pans. (Cake may sink slightly in center.) Fill and spread side and top of cake with Apricot Glaze. Spread side and top of torte with Dark Chocolate Glaze. When glaze is set, pipe edges of torte with sweetened whipped cream if desired. Refrigerate in airtight container. Bring to room temperature before serving.

Apricot Glaze

Heat contents of 1 jar (12 ounces) apricot jam in saucepan to boiling. Simmer 5 minutes; cool completely.

Dark Chocolate Glaze

Heat 3 squares (1 ounce each) semisweet chocolate over low heat, stirring frequently, until melted. Add ½ cup margarine or butter; stir until margarine is melted. Cool to room temperature and until slightly thickened.

Chocolate Mousse Cake

1 cup sugar
2 cups margarine or butter
1 cup water
1 teaspoon instant coffee, if desired
16 squares (1 ounce each) semisweet
   chocolate, cut into pieces
8 eggs, slightly beaten
½ cup chilled whipping cream
1 tablespoon powdered sugar

Heat oven to 350°. Grease a springform pan, 9 × 3 inches. Heat sugar, margarine, water, coffee and chocolate in 3-quart saucepan over low heat, stirring constantly, until melted and smooth. Remove from heat; stir in eggs. Pour into pan. Bake until wooden pick inserted in center comes out clean, 45 to 50 minutes. Cool completely. Remove side of springform pan. Cover with plastic wrap and refrigerate until chilled, at least 4 hours.

Remove plastic wrap. Beat whipping cream and powdered sugar in chilled bowl until stiff; spread over top of cake. Refrigerate any remaining cake.

NOTE: The batter is very thin. If springform pan does not fit tightly, line pan with aluminum foil.

CHOCOLATE CURLS

Place bar of milk chocolate on waxed paper. Make chocolate curls by pulling a vegetable parer toward you, pressing firmly against the chocolate in long, thin strokes. Transfer each curl carefully with a wooden pick to waxed paper-lined cookie sheet or directly onto frosted cake, pie or dessert.

The curls will be easier to make if the chocolate is slightly warm. Let the chocolate stand in a warm place for about 15 minutes before making the curls. Semisweet chocolate can be used but the curls will be smaller. Thicker bars of chocolate will make larger curls.

Peppermint Cream-filled Cake

½ cup cocoa
¾ cup boiling water
1¾ cups sugar
1½ cups all-purpose flour
1½ teaspoons baking soda
1 teaspoon salt
½ cup vegetable oil
2 teaspoons vanilla
7 egg yolks
1 cup egg whites (about 8)
½ teaspoon cream of tartar
  Peppermint Cream (right)

Heat oven to 325°. Mix cocoa and boiling water; let stand until cool. Mix sugar, flour, baking soda and salt in 3-quart bowl. Beat in cocoa mixture, oil, vanilla and egg yolks with spoon until smooth. Beat egg whites and cream of tartar in 3-quart bowl on medium speed until stiff peaks form. Pour egg yolk mixture gradually over beaten egg whites, folding with rubber spatula just until blended. Pour into ungreased tube pan, 10 × 4 inches.

Bake until top springs back when touched lightly, about 1¼ hours. Invert pan on heat-proof funnel; let hang until cake is cold.

Remove cake from pan; place cake upside down. Slice off top of cake about 1 inch down; reserve top. Make cuts down into cake 1 inch from outer edge and 1 inch from edge of hole, leaving substantial "walls" on each side. Remove cake within cuts with a spoon or curved knife, being careful to leave a base of cake 1 inch thick.

Prepare Peppermint Cream; spoon half of the mixture into cake cavity. Press mixture firmly into cavity. Replace top of cake; press gently. Frost side and top of cake with remaining Peppermint Cream. Just before serving garnish with Chocolate Leaves (below) or crushed peppermint candy if desired. Refrigerate any remaining cake.

Peppermint Cream

1 cup powdered sugar
2 cups chilled whipping cream
1 teaspoon peppermint extract
6 to 8 drops red food color

Beat all ingredients in chilled bowl until stiff.

CHOCOLATE LEAVES

Wash and dry 12 to 18 fresh leaves (such as rose leaves) or pliable plastic leaves. Heat ½ cup semisweet chocolate chips or 2 squares (1 ounce each) semisweet chocolate and 1 teaspoon shortening over low heat until melted. Brush chocolate about ⅛ inch thick over backs of leaves. Refrigerate until firm, at least 1 hour. Peel off leaves. Refrigerate until ready to use.

Angel Food Waldorf

1 10-inch angel food cake
3 cups chilled whipping cream
1½ cups powdered sugar
¾ cup cocoa
¼ teaspoon salt
⅔ cup toasted slivered almonds

Place cake upside down on plate or waxed paper. Slice off top of cake about 1 inch down; reserve top. Make cuts down into cake 1 inch from outer edge and 1 inch from edge of hole, leaving substantial "walls" on each side. Remove cake within cuts, with a curved knife or spoon, being careful to leave a base of cake 1 inch thick.

Beat whipping cream, powdered sugar, cocoa and salt in chilled bowl until stiff. Divide whipped cream mixture in half. Fold ⅓ cup toasted slivered almonds into half the whipped cream mixture; spoon into cake cavity. Press mixture firmly into cavity to avoid "holes" in cut slices. Replace top of cake and press gently. Frost cake with remaining whipped cream mixture. Sprinkle with ⅓ cup toasted slivered almonds. Refrigerate any remaining cake.

Chocolate Cream Roll

3 eggs
1 cup granulated sugar
⅓ cup water
1 teaspoon vanilla
¾ cup all-purpose flour
¼ cup cocoa
1 teaspoon baking powder
¼ teaspoon salt
　 Powdered sugar
　 Cocoa Whipped Cream (right)

Heat oven to 375°. Line jelly roll pan, 15½ × 10½ × 1 inch, with aluminum foil or waxed paper; grease generously. Beat eggs in 1½-quart bowl on high speed until very thick and lemon colored, about 5 minutes. Pour eggs into 2½-quart bowl. Beat in granulated sugar gradually. Beat in water and vanilla on low speed. Add flour, cocoa, baking powder and salt gradually, beating just until batter is smooth. Pour into pan.

Bake until wooden pick inserted in center comes out clean, 12 to 15 minutes. Immediately loosen cake from edges of pan; invert on towel sprinkled generously with powdered sugar. Carefully remove foil; trim off stiff edges if necessary.

While hot, roll cake and towel from narrow end. Cool on wire rack at least 30 minutes. Unroll cake; remove towel. Spread with Cocoa Whipped Cream. Roll up; sprinkle with powdered sugar. Refrigerate.

Cocoa Whipped Cream

1 cup chilled whipping cream
¼ cup powdered sugar
2 tablespoons cocoa
½ teaspoon vanilla

Beat cream, sugar and cocoa in chilled 2-quart bowl until stiff. Beat in vanilla.

CHOCOLATE-MINT ROLL: Omit Cocoa Whipped Cream. Spread 1 pint vanilla ice cream, softened, on cake; sprinkle with ¼ cup crushed peppermint candy. Roll up; wrap in plastic wrap. Freeze until firm, about 6 hours. If desired, sprinkle roll with powdered sugar.

CHERRY-ALMOND ROLL: Fold ¼ cup chopped maraschino cherries and ¼ cup diced toasted almonds into the Cocoa Whipped Cream.

CHOCOLATE-ALMOND ROLL: Fold ¼ cup toasted sliced almonds into the Cocoa Whipped Cream. Spread roll with whipped cream mixture. Roll up; frost with French Silk Frosting (below) Refrigerate any remaining cake roll.

FRENCH SILK FROSTING: Beat ⅓ cup margarine or butter, softened, 1⅓ cups powdered sugar, 1 square (1 ounce) unsweetened chocolate, melted and cooled and ½ teaspoon vanilla on low speed until smooth. Gradually beat in 1 tablespoon milk until fluffy and of spreading consistency.

Apricot-Chocolate Cake

3 eggs
1 cup sugar
⅓ cup water
1 teaspoon vanilla
¾ cup all-purpose flour
¼ cup cocoa
1 teaspoon baking powder
¼ teaspoon salt
1 can (17 ounces) peeled whole apricots, drained
1 jar (12 ounces) apricot preserves
1 tablespoon lemon juice
  Chocolate Frosting (right)
¼ cup almond-flavored liqueur

Heat oven to 375°. Line jelly roll pan, 15½×10½×1 inch, with aluminum foil or waxed paper; grease generously. Beat eggs in small bowl on high speed until very thick and lemon colored, about 5 minutes. Pour eggs into large bowl. Beat in sugar gradually. Beat in water and vanilla on low speed. Add flour, cocoa, baking powder and salt gradually, beating just until batter is smooth. Pour into pan, spreading batter to corners.

Bake until wooden pick inserted in center comes out clean, 12 to 15 minutes. Immediately loosen cake from edges of pan; invert on towel sprinkled generously with cocoa. Carefully remove foil; cool cake.

Cut apricots into halves and remove pits. Drain halves, cut sides down. Heat apricot preserves and lemon juice over low heat, stirring constantly, just to boiling. Prepare Chocolate Frosting.

Trim off stiff edges of cake if necessary. Cut cake crosswise into 3 equal pieces, about 10½×5 inches each. Place one piece on plate; sprinkle with 1 tablespoon liqueur. Spread about ⅓ cup frosting on cake to within ⅜ inch of edges. Spread with ⅓ cup of the apricot mixture. Repeat with second cake piece, 1 tablespoon liqueur, ⅓ cup frosting and ⅓ cup apricot mixture; top with remaining cake piece. Sprinkle cake with remaining liqueur.

Arrange apricot halves, cut sides down, on cake. Spread remaining apricot mixture over apricots. Remove 1 cup frosting; reserve. Frost sides of cake with remaining frosting. Place reserved frosting in decorators' tube or bag fitted with decorating tip; pipe border around top and bottom edges of cake. Cover loosely and store at room temperature no longer than 24 hours.

Chocolate Frosting

½ cup margarine or butter, softened
3 squares (1 ounce each) unsweetened chocolate, melted and cooled
3 cups powdered sugar
1 teaspoon vanilla
1 teaspoon almond extract
  About 3 tablespoons milk

Mix margarine and chocolate. Stir in powdered sugar. Beat in remaining ingredients until smooth and of spreading consistency.

CHOCOLATE SILHOUETTE

Place desired design on cookie sheet or flat plate. (Design can be a tracing from a magazine, atlas, coloring book or birthday card.) Cover design with waxed paper. Soften 1 packet (1 ounce) premelted chocolate in hot water and snip off tiny corner. Squeeze small amount of chocolate onto center of waxed paper over the design. Use small spatula or knife to spread chocolate within lines of design. If desired, reserve about 2 teaspoons chocolate in packet for writing a message.

Place chocolate design in freezer until firm. Remove design from waxed paper by peeling paper away; transfer design to top of frosted cake (frosting should be smooth).

White Chocolate Cake

2 tablespoons white vinegar
1 cup evaporated milk
2¼ cups all-purpose flour
1½ cups sugar
¾ cup shortening
1 teaspoon baking soda
1 teaspoon vanilla
½ teaspoon salt
4 eggs
4 ounces white chocolate (vanilla-flavored candy coating), melted and cooled slightly
1 cup flaked coconut
1 cup chopped pecans
Vanilla Glaze (below)

Heat oven to 350°. Grease and flour 12-cup bundt cake pan. Stir vinegar into milk; let stand until slightly thickened, about 1 minute. Beat vinegar mixture and remaining ingredients except coconut, pecans and glaze in 2½-quart bowl on low speed, scraping bowl constantly, 30 seconds. Beat on high speed, scraping bowl occasionally, 3 minutes. Stir in coconut and pecans. Pour into pan.

Bake until wooden pick inserted in center of cake comes out clean, 50 to 55 minutes; cool 15 minutes. Invert on wire rack or heatproof serving plate. Remove pan; cool cake completely. Prepare Vanilla Glaze; spread over top of cake, allowing some to drizzle down side. Sprinkle with chopped pecans if desired.

Vanilla Glaze

2 tablespoons margarine or butter
1 cup powdered sugar
½ teaspoon vanilla
3 to 4 teaspoons evaporated milk

Heat margarine in 1-quart saucepan over low heat until melted. Stir in powdered sugar, vanilla and milk until smooth and of desired consistency.

Chocolate Chip Pound Cake

1¾ cups all-purpose flour
1 cup sugar
¼ cup shortening
¼ cup margarine or butter, softened
¾ cup milk
2 teaspoons baking powder
1 teaspoon salt
1 teaspoon vanilla
5 egg yolks
2 squares (1 ounce each) unsweetened chocolate, grated
½ cup chopped nuts

Heat oven to 350°. Grease and flour loaf pan, 9 × 5 × 3 inches. Beat all ingredients except chocolate and nuts on low speed, scraping bowl constantly, 30 seconds. Beat on medium speed, scraping bowl frequently, 2 minutes. Stir in chocolate and nuts. Pour into pan.

Bake until wooden pick inserted in center comes out clean, 65 to 70 minutes. Cool 10 minutes; remove from pan.

CHOCOLATE-DIPPED BANANA SLICES

Cut 1 medium banana diagonally into ¼-inch slices. Dip slices into lemon juice; drain. Heat ½ cup semisweet chocolate chips and 1 teaspoon shortening over low heat, stirring occasionally, until chocolate is melted. Cool slightly. Dip half of each banana slice into chocolate mixture; place on waxed paper. Refrigerate until set. Arrange around top edge of frosted cake.

Double Chocolate Pie, Banana-Peanut Pie

Double Chocolate Pie

9-inch Baked Pie Shell (page 41)
1½ cups sugar
⅓ cup cornstarch
½ teaspoon salt
3 cups milk
1 package (6 ounces) semisweet chocolate
    chips
2 squares (1 ounce each) unsweetened
    chocolate, coarsely chopped
4 egg yolks, slightly beaten
1 tablespoon vanilla
    Sweetened Whipped Cream

Bake pie shell; cool. Mix sugar, cornstarch and salt in 2-quart saucepan. Stir in milk gradually; stir in chocolate chips and unsweetened chocolate. Cook over medium heat, stirring constantly, until mixture thickens and boils. Boil and stir 1 minute. Stir at least half of the hot mixture gradually into egg yolks. Blend into hot mixture in saucepan. Boil and stir 1 minute. Remove from heat; stir in vanilla. Pour into pie shell; press plastic wrap on filling. Refrigerate at least 4 hours but no longer than 48 hours. Remove plastic wrap; top pie with whipped cream.

CHOCOLATE CREAM PIE: Omit chocolate chips and increase the vanilla to 1 tablespoon plus 1 teaspoon.

Banana-Peanut Pie

Nutty Graham Cracker Crust (below)
1 package (about 3½ ounces) regular chocolate
    pudding and pie filling
½ cup chunky peanut butter
2 medium bananas

Prepare Nutty Graham Cracker Crust. Prepare pudding and pie filling as directed on package for pie filling except — decrease milk to 1¾ cups. Remove from heat; stir in peanut butter thoroughly. Let stand, stirring occasionally, 5 minutes.

Slice bananas thinly into pie shell. Pour filling over bananas; press plastic wrap onto filling. Refrigerate until firm, at least 3 hours but no longer than 48 hours. Remove plastic wrap; garnish with whipped cream and Chocolate-dipped Banana Slices (page 32) if desired.

Nutty Graham Cracker Crust

1½ cups graham cracker crumbs (about 20
    squares)
⅓ cup margarine or butter, melted
¼ cup finely chopped salted peanuts, if
    desired

Heat oven to 350°. Mix cracker crumbs, margarine and peanuts. Press firmly and evenly against bottom and side of ungreased pie plate, 9 × 1¼ inches. Bake 10 minutes; cool.

Butter Crunch Chocolate Pie

1 cup all-purpose flour
½ cup chopped pecans, walnuts or coconut
½ cup margarine or butter
¼ cup packed brown sugar
1 package (5⅛ ounces) regular chocolate flavor pudding and pie filling
Meringue (below)

Heat oven to 400°. Mix flour, pecans, margarine and brown sugar with hands. Spread in ungreased rectangular pan, 13 × 9 × 2 inches. Bake 15 minutes; stir.

Press 2 cups hot pecan mixture against bottom and sides of ungreased pie plate, 9 × 1¼ inches. Prepare pudding and pie filling as directed on package for pie filling. Prepare Meringue. Pour hot pudding into pie plate. Immediately top with meringue. Bake in 375° oven until delicate brown, 15 to 20 minutes; cool. Top with remaining pecan mixture if desired.

Meringue

3 egg whites
¼ teaspoon cream of tartar
⅓ cup sugar

Beat egg whites with cream of tartar in 1½-quart bowl until foamy. Gradually beat in sugar. Continue beating until stiff and glossy. Do not underbeat.

Strawberry Sour Cream Pie

Graham Cracker Crust (below)
1 cup dairy sour cream
1 cup milk
1 package (4 ounces) chocolate flavor instant pudding and pie filling
1½ cups sliced strawberries
Strawberry Glacé (below)

Prepare Graham Cracker Crust. Beat sour cream and milk with hand beater until smooth. Mix in pudding and pie filling (dry) until smooth and slightly thickened. Pour into crust. Arrange sliced strawberries over filling. Pour Strawberry Glacé over strawberries. Refrigerate until firm, about 2 hours. Top with whipped cream if desired.

Graham Cracker Crust

Heat oven to 350°. Mix 1½ cups graham cracker crumbs (about 20 squares), 3 tablespoons sugar and ⅓ cup margarine or butter, melted. Press firmly and evenly against bottom and side of ungreased pie plate, 9 × 1¼ inches. Bake 10 minutes; cool.

Strawberry Glacé

½ cup sliced strawberries
¼ cup water
½ cup sugar
1 tablespoon plus 1½ teaspoons cornstarch
¼ cup water

Heat sliced strawberries and ¼ cup water in small saucepan; simmer about 3 minutes. Mix sugar and cornstarch in small bowl; stir in ¼ cup water. Stir into hot strawberry mixture. Cook, stirring constantly, until mixture thickens and boils. Boil and stir 1 minute; cool.

BANANA SOUR CREAM PIE: Omit Strawberry Glacé. Slice 2 or 3 bananas into crust. Pour sour cream-pudding mixture over bananas. Just before serving, top with sweetened whipped cream and additional banana slices.

Peanut Butter Pie

9-inch Unbaked Pie Shell (page 41)
²/₃ *cup sugar*
¹/₃ *cup creamy peanut butter*
1 *cup dark corn syrup*
¹/₂ *teaspoon salt*
3 *eggs*
1 *cup salted peanuts*
1 *package (6 ounces) semisweet chocolate*
   chips
   Sweetened Whipped Cream

Prepare pie shell. Heat oven to 375°. Beat sugar, peanut butter, corn syrup, salt and eggs on low speed until smooth; stir in peanuts. Pour into pastry-lined pie plate; sprinkle with chocolate chips.

Bake until crust is golden brown, 40 to 50 minutes. (Center of filling may be slightly soft but will become firm as pie cools.) Cool 30 minutes. Refrigerate until chilled, at least 3 hours but no longer than 24 hours. Serve with whipped cream.

Chocolate-Pecan Pie

9-inch Unbaked Pie Shell (page 41)
¹/₃ *cup margarine or butter*
2 *squares (1 ounce each) unsweetened*
   chocolate
3 *eggs*
²/₃ *cup sugar*
¹/₂ *teaspoon salt*
1 *cup corn syrup*
1 *cup pecan halves or broken pieces*

Prepare pie shell. Heat oven to 375°. Heat margarine and chocolate over low heat, stirring constantly, until chocolate is melted; cool slightly. Beat eggs, sugar, salt, chocolate mixture and syrup with hand beater. Stir in pecans. Pour into pie shell.

Bake until set, 40 to 50 minutes. Cool slightly. Serve warm or refrigerate. Serve with sweetened whipped cream if desired. Refrigerate any remaining pie.

Brownie Pie

9-inch Unbaked Pie Shell (page 41)
¹/₂ *cup cocoa*
¹/₂ *cup sugar*
¹/₄ *cup margarine or butter, melted*
³/₄ *cup dark corn syrup*
3 *eggs*
³/₄ *cup coarsely chopped walnuts*

Prepare pie shell. Heat oven to 375°. Mix cocoa and sugar. Beat sugar mixture, margarine, syrup and eggs with hand beater. Stir in walnuts. Pour into pie shell. Bake just until set, 40 to 50 minutes. Serve slightly warm or cold with ice cream or whipped cream if desired.

Cocoa Bavarian Pie

8-inch Baked Pie Shell (page 41)
1 *envelope (1 tablespoon) unflavored*
   gelatin
¹/₄ *cup cold water*
1 *cup powdered sugar*
¹/₂ *cup cocoa*
2 *cups chilled whipping cream*
1 *teaspoon vanilla*
¹/₈ *teaspoon salt*

Bake pie shell; cool. Sprinkle gelatin on cold water in saucepan to soften; heat over low heat, stirring constantly, until gelatin is dissolved. Mix all ingredients (except gelatin); beat until mixture begins to thicken. Gradually add dissolved gelatin. Beat until mixture holds a soft peak. Pour into pie shell; refrigerate until set, at least 1 hour. Garnish with sweetened whipped cream and Chocolate Cut-outs (page 38) if desired.

MARBLE PIE: Follow recipe above — except use only 1½ cups chilled whipping cream. Beat remaining ½ cup whipping cream in chilled bowl until stiff; put spoonfuls over top of chocolate mixture in pie shell. Run spatula or knife through filling to marble the top.

Rum Cheese Pie

9-inch Baked Pie Shell (page 41)
1 *package (8 ounces) cream cheese,*
  softened
1 *can (14 ounces) sweetened condensed*
  milk
2 *eggs, separated*
1/4 *teaspoon cream of tartar*
1/2 *cup sugar*
1 *square (1 ounce) unsweetened chocolate*
1 *tablespoon rum or 1 teaspoon rum*
  flavoring

Bake pie shell; cool. Beat cream cheese until light and fluffy; gradually beat in sweetened condensed milk and egg yolks until well blended. Cook over low heat, stirring constantly, until mixture begins to thicken; cool slightly. Beat egg whites and cream of tartar until foamy. Gradually beat in sugar; continue beating until stiff and glossy. Fold milk mixture into egg whites.

Heat chocolate until melted; fold into 1½ cups of the milk mixture. Spread on bottom of pie shell. Fold rum into remaining milk mixture; spread over chocolate layer. Refrigerate until chilled. Garnish with sweetened whipped cream and grated chocolate (page 26) if desired. Refrigerate any remaining pie.

Angel Pie

2 *egg whites*
1/8 *teaspoon cream of tartar*
1/2 *cup sugar*
1/2 *cup chopped nuts*
1 *bar (4 ounces) sweet chocolate or*
  6-ounce package semisweet chocolate chips
3 *tablespoons water*
1 *teaspoon vanilla*
1 *cup chilled whipping cream*

Heat oven to 275°. Lightly grease pie plate, 8 × 1¼ inches. Beat egg whites and cream of tartar until foamy. Beat in sugar gradually; continue beating until mixture holds stiff peaks. Do not underbeat. Fold in chopped

nuts. Spread in pie plate, making a nest-like shell by building sides up above edge of pie plate. Bake 45 minutes. Turn off oven; leave meringue in oven with door closed 45 minutes. Remove from oven; cool.

Heat chocolate and water in saucepan over low heat until chocolate is melted; cool. Stir in vanilla. Beat whipping cream in chilled bowl until stiff. Fold chocolate into whipped cream. Spoon into meringue shell. Refrigerate at least 12 hours, but no longer than 24 hours. Garnish with whipped cream, chopped nuts or grated chocolate (page 26) if desired.

Classic French Silk Pie

9-inch Baked Pie Shell (page 41)
1 *cup sugar*
3/4 *cup margarine or butter, softened*
3 *squares (1 ounce each) unsweetened*
  chocolate, melted and cooled
1½ *teaspoons instant coffee*
1/4 *teaspoon cream of tartar*
1½ *teaspoons vanilla*
3 *eggs*
1 *cup chilled whipping cream*
2 *tablespoons powdered sugar*

Bake pie shell; cool. Beat sugar and margarine in a 1½ quart bowl until light and fluffy. Stir in chocolate, coffee, cream of tartar and vanilla. Beat in eggs until light and fluffy, about 3 minutes. Pour into baked pie shell. Refrigerate until set, 3 to 4 hours or cover with plastic wrap and freeze at least 8 hours.

If pie is frozen, remove from freezer 15 minutes before serving. Beat whipping cream and powdered sugar in chilled bowl until stiff. Top pie with whipped cream and, if desired, Chocolate Curls (page 27) or chopped nuts.

NOTE: Chocolate can be decreased to 1 square (1 ounce) if desired. Chocolate flavor will be milder and coffee flavor will be slightly more pronounced.

Classic French Silk Pie

Chocolate Chiffon Pie

9-inch Baked Pie Shell (page 41)
½ cup sugar
1 envelope unflavored gelatin
½ teaspoon salt
1⅓ cups water
2 squares (1 ounce each) unsweetened
    chocolate, melted
3 eggs, separated
1 teaspoon vanilla
¼ teaspoon cream of tartar
½ cup sugar
½ cup chilled whipping cream

Bake pie shell; cool. Stir together ½ cup sugar, the gelatin and salt in small saucepan; stir in water and chocolate. Cook over medium heat, stirring constantly, until blended; remove from heat. Beat egg yolks slightly; stir chocolate mixture slowly into yolks. Return mixture to saucepan. Cook over medium heat, stirring constantly, just until mixture boils. Place pan in bowl of ice and water or refrigerate, stirring occasionally, until mixture mounds slightly when dropped from a spoon. Stir in vanilla.

Beat egg whites and cream of tartar until foamy. Beat in ½ cup sugar, 1 tablespoon at a time; continue beating until stiff and glossy. Do not underbeat. Fold chocolate mixture into meringue. Beat whipping cream in chilled bowl until stiff. Fold into chocolate meringue. Pile into pie shell. Refrigerate at least 3 hours or until set. Garnish with Cocoa Fluff Topping (page 80) and Grated Chocolate (page 26) if desired. Refrigerate any remaining pie

---

CHOCOLATE CUT-OUTS

Heat 1 bar (4 ounces) sweet cooking chocolate or 4 squares (1 ounce each) semisweet chocolate over low heat, stirring frequently, until melted. Spread over outside bottom of square pan, 8 × 8 × 2 inches. Refrigerate until firm; bring to room temperature. Cut into circles, stars, diamonds or other desired shapes. Refrigerate until ready to place on frosted cake or pie.

Peppermint-Chocolate Pie

Chocolate Cookie Crust (below)
½ cup milk
24 large marshmallows
¼ teaspoon peppermint extract
⅛ teaspoon salt
6 drops red food color
1 cup chilled whipping cream
    Chocolate Topping (below)
2 tablespoons crushed peppermint candy

Prepare Chocolate Cookie Crust. Heat milk and marshmallows over low heat, stirring constantly, just until marshmallows are melted. Remove from heat; stir in peppermint extract, salt and food color. Place pan in bowl of ice and water or refrigerate, stirring occasionally, until mixture mounds slightly when dropped from a spoon.

Beat whipping cream in chilled 1½-quart bowl until stiff. Stir marshmallow mixture until blended; fold into whipped cream. Pour into crust. Refrigerate until set, at least 2 hours. Prepare Chocolate Topping; drizzle over pie. Sprinkle with candy just before serving.

Chocolate Cookie Crust

Heat oven to 350°. Mix 1½ cups chocolate wafer crumbs and ¼ cup margarine or butter, melted. Press firmly and evenly against bottom and side of ungreased pie plate, 9 × 1¼ inches. Bake 10 minutes; cool.

Chocolate Topping

½ cup semisweet chocolate chips
3 tablespoons milk
1 tablespoon margarine or butter
½ cup powdered sugar

Heat chocolate chips, milk and margarine over low heat, stirring constantly, until chocolate chips and margarine are melted. Remove from heat; stir in powdered sugar. Beat until smooth and glossy.

Coconut Chocolate Pie

Coconut Chocolate Crust (below)
1½ cups miniature marshmallows or 16 large marshmallows
½ cup milk
1 bar (8 ounces) milk chocolate
1 cup chilled whipping cream
Toasted flaked coconut

Prepare Coconut Chocolate Crust. Heat marshmallows, milk and chocolate over low heat, stirring constantly, until chocolate and marshmallows are melted. Place pan in bowl of ice and water or refrigerate, stirring occasionally, until mixture mounds slightly when dropped from a spoon. Beat whipping cream in chilled bowl until stiff; fold chocolate mixture into whipped cream. Pour into Coconut Chocolate Crust; sprinkle with coconut. Refrigerate at least 8 hours or until set. Cut into small wedges.

NOTE: 9-inch Baked Pie Shell (page 41) or Graham Cracker Crust (page 34) can be substituted for the Coconut Chocolate Crust.

Coconut Chocolate Crust

2 squares (1 ounce each) unsweetened chocolate
2 tablespoons margarine or butter
1½ cups flaked coconut
⅔ cup powdered sugar
2 tablespoons milk

Grease pie plate, 9 × 1¼ inches, with margarine or butter, softened. Heat chocolate and margarine in small saucepan over low heat until melted. Add coconut, sugar and milk; mix thoroughly. Press mixture firmly and evenly against side and bottom of pie plate. Refrigerate at least 2 hours.

Brandy Alexander Pie

Chocolate Cookie Crust (page 38)
3 cups miniature marshmallows or 32 large marshmallows
½ cup milk
¼ cup dark crème de cacao
3 tablespoons brandy
1½ cups chilled whipping cream

Prepare Chocolate Cookie Crust. Heat marshmallows and milk in 3-quart saucepan over low heat, stirring constantly, until marshmallows are melted. Place pan in bowl of ice and water or refrigerate, stirring occasionally, until mixture mounds slightly when dropped from a spoon. Beat whipping cream in chilled 2½-quart bowl until stiff. Stir marshmallow mixture until blended; stir in liqueurs. Fold into whipped cream. Pour into crust. Sprinkle grated semisweet chocolate over top if desired. Refrigerate until set, at least 4 hours.

CHERRY CORDIAL PIE: Substitute ½ cup cherry liqueur for the crème de cacao and brandy. Fold in a few drops red food color if desired.

GRASSHOPPER PIE: Substitute ¼ cup crème de menthe for the dark crème de cacao and 3 tablespoons white crème de cacao for the brandy. Fold in a few drops green food color if desired.

SHAVED CHOCOLATE

Unsweetened, semisweet or sweet chocolate can be used for shaved chocolate. Slide a vegetable parer across the surface of the chocolate, using short, quick strokes. Sprinkle the shaved chocolate on frosted cakes, pies and desserts as a garnish.

Fudgy Mocha Pie

Fudgy Mocha Pie

  4 egg whites
 1/4 teaspoon cream of tartar
 3/4 cup granulated sugar
  3 tablespoons cocoa
 3/4 cup powdered sugar
 1/3 cup cocoa
1 1/2 cups chilled whipping cream
  2 tablespoons coffee-flavored liqueur

Heat oven to 275°. Lightly grease pie plate, 9 × 1 1/4 inches. Beat egg whites and cream of tartar in large bowl until foamy. Beat in granulated sugar, 1 tablespoon at a time; continue beating until stiff and glossy. Do not underbeat. Beat in 3 tablespoons cocoa on low speed just until blended. Spoon into pie plate, pressing meringue against bottom and side.

Bake 1 hour. Turn off oven; leave meringue in oven with door closed 1 hour. Remove from oven; finish cooling away from draft.

Beat powdered sugar, 1/3 cup cocoa, the whipping cream and liqueur in chilled 2 1/2-quart bowl until stiff. Spread in pie shell. Freeze at least 12 hours but no longer than 48 hours. Garnish with additional sweetened whipped cream, and sprinkle with sliced or chopped almonds if desired.

Coffee Sundae Pie

    Chocolate Cookie Crust (page 38)
  1 quart coffee ice cream
  1 pint pistachio, butter pecan or French vanilla ice cream
 1/4 cup dark crème de cacao or chocolate-flavored syrup

Prepare Chocolate Cookie Crust. Pack coffee ice cream into crust. Freeze until firm, at least 1 hour. At serving time, place scoop of pistachio ice cream on each serving and drizzle with 1 or 2 teaspoons crème de cacao.

CHOCOLATE SUNDAE PIE: Substitute chocolate ice cream for the coffee ice cream and top with French vanilla ice cream. Substitute crème de menthe syrup for the crème de cacao.

Crunchy Nut Ice-Cream Pie

1½ cups ground pecans, walnuts or
      almonds
  3 tablespoons sugar
  2 tablespoons margarine or butter,
      softened
  1 quart coffee, chocolate or vanilla ice
      cream
      Rich Chocolate Sauce (page 80)

Heat oven to 400°. Mix pecans, sugar and margarine. Press firmly and evenly against bottom and side of ungreased pie plate, 9 × 1¼ inches. Bake 6 to 8 minutes; cool.

Spoon or scoop ice cream into pie shell. Freeze until firm, about 4 hours. Remove from freezer 10 to 15 minutes before serving. Cut into wedges; spoon Rich Chocolate Sauce over each serving.

8- or 9-inch Unbaked Pie Shell

⅓ cup plus 1 tablespoon shortening or ⅓ cup
      lard
  1 cup all-purpose flour
½ teaspoon salt
  2 to 3 tablespoons cold water

Cut shortening into flour until particles are size of tiny peas. Sprinkle in water, 1 tablespoon at a time, tossing with a fork until all flour is moistened and pastry almost cleans side of bowl (1 to 2 teaspoons water can be added if necessary).

Gather pastry into a ball. Shape into a flattened round on lightly floured cloth-covered board. Roll pastry from center to outside evenly in all directions 2 inches larger than inverted pie plate with floured cloth-covered rolling pin. Fold pastry in quarters; unfold and ease into pie plate, pressing firmly against bottom and side.

Trim overhanging edge of pastry 1 inch from rim of pan. Fold and roll pastry under, even with plate (see below). Flute edge (see below). Fill and bake as directed in recipe.

8- OR 9-INCH BAKED PIE SHELL: Heat oven to 475°. Follow directions for Unbaked Pie Shell (left) except — prick bottom and side thoroughly with fork. Bake until light brown, 8 to 10 minutes; cool.

Fluted Pastry Edges

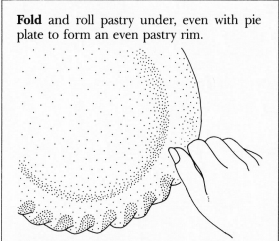

Fold and roll pastry under, even with pie plate to form an even pastry rim.

Rope Edge: Place thumb on pastry rim at an angle. Pinch pastry by pressing knuckle down into pastry toward thumb. Repeat along entire edge.

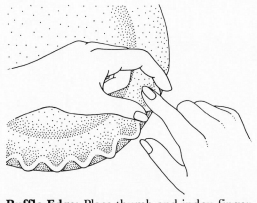

Ruffle Edge: Place thumb and index finger about one inch apart on pastry rim. With other index finger, pull pastry toward outside. Repeat along entire edge.

Cookies

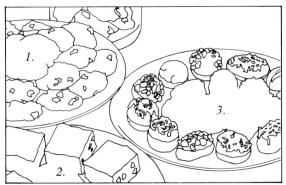

1. *Chocolate Chip Cookies*, 2. *Deluxe Brownies*, 3. *Bonbon Cookies*

Chocolate Chip Cookies

1 cup margarine or butter, softened
3/4 cup granulated sugar
3/4 cup packed brown sugar
1 egg
2 1/4 cups all-purpose flour
1 teaspoon baking soda
1/2 teaspoon salt
1 cup coarsely chopped nuts
1 package (12 ounces) semisweet chocolate chips

Heat oven to 375°. Mix margarine, sugars and egg thoroughly. Stir in flour, baking soda and salt (dough will be stiff). Stir in nuts and chocolate chips. Drop dough by rounded teaspoonfuls about 2 inches apart onto ungreased cookie sheet. Bake until light brown, 8 to 10 minutes. (Centers will be soft.) Cool slightly before removing from cookie sheet. About 6 dozen cookies.

CRISP CHOCOLATE CHIP COOKIES: Decrease flour to 2 cups. About 5 dozen cookies.

JUMBO CHOCOLATE CHIP COOKIES: Drop dough by 1/4 cupfuls about 3 inches apart onto ungreased cookie sheet. Bake until edges are set, 12 to 15 minutes. Cool before removing from cookie sheet. About 1 1/2 dozen cookies.

CHOCOLATE CHIP BARS: Press dough evenly in ungreased rectangular pan, 13 × 9 × 2 inches. Bake until golden brown, about 25 minutes; cool. Cut into bars, about 3 × 1 1/2 inches. 24 bars.

Cherry-Chocolate Jumbles

2 3/4 cups all-purpose flour
1 1/2 cups packed brown sugar
1 cup dairy sour cream
1/2 cup shortening
1 teaspoon salt
1 teaspoon vanilla
1/2 teaspoon baking soda
2 eggs
1 cup chopped nuts, if desired
1/2 cup semisweet chocolate chips
1/2 cup cut-up maraschino cherries
Browned Butter Glaze (below)

Mix all ingredients except nuts, chocolate chips, cherries and glaze in 2 1/2-quart bowl. Stir in nuts, chocolate chips and cherries. If dough is soft, cover and refrigerate. Heat oven to 375°. Drop dough by rounded teaspoonfuls about 2 inches apart onto ungreased cookie sheet. Bake until almost no indentation remains when touched, about 10 minutes. Immediately remove from cookie sheet; cool. Spread with Browned Butter Glaze. 4 1/2 to 5 dozen cookies.

Browned Butter Glaze

Heat 1/3 cup margarine or butter over low heat until golden brown. Remove from heat; stir in 2 cups powdered sugar, 1 1/2 teaspoons vanilla and 2 to 4 tablespoons hot water until smooth and of desired consistency.

CHERRY-COCONUT JUMBLES: Omit nuts and stir in 1 cup shredded coconut.

CHERRY-RAISIN JUMBLES: Substitute 1 cup raisins for the nuts.

CHERRY-PEANUT JUMBLES: Substitute 1 cup salted peanuts for the nuts.

CHOCOLATE CHIP JUMBLES: Omit cherries and stir in 1 package (6 ounces) semisweet chocolate chips.

Chocolate Drop Cookies

1   cup sugar
½   cup margarine or butter, softened
⅓   cup buttermilk or water
1   teaspoon vanilla
1   egg
2   squares (1 ounce each) unsweetened
     chocolate, melted and cooled
1¾ cups all-purpose flour
½   teaspoon baking soda
½   teaspoon salt
1   cup chopped nuts, if desired
     Chocolate Frosting or Browned Butter
     Frosting (below)

Heat oven to 400°. Mix sugar, margarine, buttermilk, vanilla, egg and chocolate in 2½-quart bowl. Stir in flour, baking soda and salt. Stir in nuts. Drop dough by rounded teaspoonfuls about 2 inches apart onto ungreased cookie sheet. Bake until almost no indentation remains when touched, 8 to 10 minutes. Immediately remove from cookie sheet; cool. Frost with Chocolate Frosting. About 4½ dozen cookies.

Chocolate Frosting

Heat 2 squares (1 ounce each) unsweetened chocolate and 2 tablespoons margarine or butter over low heat until melted. Remove from heat; stir in 3 tablespoons water and about 2 cups powdered sugar until smooth and of spreading consistency.

Browned Butter Frosting

Heat ¼ cup margarine or butter over low heat until golden brown. Remove from heat; stir in 2 cups powdered sugar, 1 teaspoon vanilla and about 2 tablespoons half-and-half until smooth and of spreading consistency.

CHERRY DROP COOKIES: Omit nuts. Stir in 2 cups cut-up candied or maraschino cherries. Use Chocolate Frosting.

COCOA DROP COOKIES: Increase margarine to ⅔ cup; omit chocolate and stir in ½ cup cocoa.

Chocolate Drop Cookies

Double Chocolate Oatmeal Cookies

1½ cups sugar
1 cup margarine or butter, softened
¼ cup water
1 teaspoon vanilla
1 egg
3 cups quick-cooking oats
1¼ cups all-purpose flour
⅓ cup cocoa
½ teaspoon baking soda
½ teaspoon salt
1 package (6 ounces) semisweet chocolate chips

Heat oven to 350°. Mix sugar, margarine, water, vanilla and egg in 2½-quart bowl. Stir in remaining ingredients. Drop dough by rounded teaspoonfuls about 2 inches apart onto ungreased cookie sheet. Bake until almost no indentation remains when touched, 10 to 12 minutes. Immediately remove from cookie sheet. About 5½ dozen cookies.

Rocky Road Cookies

1 package (6 ounces) semisweet chocolate chips
½ cup margarine or butter
1½ cups all-purpose flour
1 cup sugar
½ teaspoon baking powder
½ teaspoon vanilla
¼ teaspoon salt
2 eggs
1 cup chopped nuts
About 4 dozen miniature marshmallows

Heat ½ cup of the chocolate chips and the margarine over low heat until melted; cool. Heat oven to 400°. Mix remaining chocolate chips, the chocolate mixture and remaining ingredients except marshmallows. Drop dough by rounded teaspoonfuls about 2 inches apart onto ungreased cookie sheet. Press a marshmallow in center of each. Bake until almost no indentation remains when touched,

Rocky Road Cookies, Double Chocolate Oatmeal Cookies, Florentines, Cherry-Chocolate Cookies

about 8 minutes. Immediately remove from cookie sheet. About 4 dozen cookies.

CHERRY-CHOCOLATE COOKIES: Substitute candied cherry halves for the miniature marshmallows.

Florentines

¼ cup sugar
¾ cup whipping cream
¼ cup all-purpose flour
½ cup slivered almonds, very finely chopped
8 ounces candied orange peel, very finely chopped
2 bars (4 ounces each) sweet cooking chocolate, cut into pieces

Heat oven to 350°. Blend sugar and cream. Stir in flour, almonds and orange peel. (Mixture will be thin.) Drop by teaspoonfuls onto heavily greased and floured cookie sheet. Spread mixture into thin circles with knife or spatula.

Bake just until edges are light brown, 10 to 12 minutes. Let cool a few minutes before removing from cookie sheet; cool. Melt chocolate over low heat, stirring constantly, until melted. Turn cookies upside down; spread with chocolate. Let stand at room temperature until chocolate is firm, at least 3 hours. Store in covered container at room temperature or refrigerate. About 5 dozen cookies.

STORING COOKIES

Store crisp, thin cookies in a loosely covered container in a dry climate; tightly covered container in a damp, humid climate. If they soften, recrisp by placing in a 300° oven for 3 to 5 minutes. Store soft, unfrosted cookies in a tightly covered container. If changed frequently, a piece of bread or apple placed in the container helps keep the cookies soft.

Coconut Meringue Cookies

    4 egg whites (½ cup)
1¼ cups sugar
    ¼ teaspoon salt
    ½ teaspoon vanilla
2½ cups shredded or flaked coconut
    2 squares (1 ounce each) unsweetened
         chocolate, melted and cooled

Heat oven to 325°. Beat egg whites in 2½-quart bowl on high speed until foamy. Beat in sugar gradually; continue beating until stiff and glossy. (Do not underbeat.) Stir in remaining ingredients. Drop mixture by heaping tea-spoonfuls about 2 inches apart onto waxed paper-covered or lightly greased cookie sheet. Bake until set and delicate brown, about 20 minutes. Immediately remove from waxed paper. About 3 dozen cookies.

NUT MERINGUE COOKIES: Substitute 2 cups finely chopped nuts for the coconut.

Coconut Chews

    2 cans (3½ ounces each) flaked coconut
         (2⅔ cups)
    ⅔ cup all-purpose flour
    ½ teaspoon salt
    1 cup chocolate-flavored syrup
    2 teaspoons vanilla

Heat oven to 375°. Mix coconut, flour and salt; stir in syrup and vanilla. Drop by rounded teaspoonfuls onto lightly greased cookie sheet. Bake until slightly firm, about 10 minutes. Immediately remove from cookie sheet. About 2½ dozen cookes.

Fruit-filled Brownies

    ⅔ cup shortening
    4 squares (1 ounce each) unsweetened
         chocolate
    2 cups sugar
    4 eggs
1½ cups all-purpose flour
    1 teaspoon baking powder
    1 teaspoon salt
         Apricot or peach preserves or orange
         marmalade
         Quick Chocolate Frosting (below)

Heat oven to 350°. Line jelly roll pan, 15½ × 10½ × 1 inch, with aluminum foil; grease. Heat shortening and chocolate in 3-quart saucepan over low heat, stirring con-stantly, until melted. Remove from heat; beat in sugar and eggs until smooth. Stir in flour, baking powder and salt. Spread in pan. Bake until slight indentation remains when touched, about 20 minutes; cool.

Remove brownies from pan; remove alumi-num foil. Cut ¼-inch strip from each long side of brownies; cut ¾-inch strip from each end. Discard strips. Cut remaining piece of brown-ies crosswise into halves. Spread 1 half with preserves; top with remaining half. Spread top with Quick Chocolate Frosting. Cut into bars, about 2 × 1 inch. 35 brownies.

Quick Chocolate Frosting

Heat 1 bar (4 ounces) sweet cooking chocolate over low heat, stirring constantly, until melted.

FREEZING COOKIES

Both frosted and unfrosted cookies can be frozen and stored from 3 to 4 months. Arrange baked cookies in a sturdy box lined with plastic wrap or aluminum foil; separate layers with wrap. Seal wrap. Close box, label and freeze. Thaw cookies by allowing them to stand uncovered on serving plate for about 20 minutes.

Fudgy Brownies

 1/2 cup margarine or butter
 1 package (12 ounces) semisweet chocolate
   chips
12/3 cups sugar
11/4 cups all-purpose flour
 1 teaspoon vanilla
 1/2 teaspoon baking powder
 1/2 teaspoon salt
 3 eggs
 1 cup chopped nuts, if desired

Heat oven to 350°. Heat margarine and chocolate chips in 3-quart saucepan over low heat, stirring constantly, until melted. Beat in remaining ingredients except nuts until smooth; stir in nuts. Spread in greased rectangular pan, 13 × 9 × 2 inches.

Bake until center is set, about 30 minutes; cool completely. Cut into bars, about 2 × 1 1/2 inches. 36 brownies.

Deluxe Brownies

 2/3 cup margarine or butter
 5 squares (1 ounce each) unsweetened
   chocolate, cut into pieces
13/4 cups sugar
 2 teaspoons vanilla
 3 eggs
 1 cup all-purpose flour
 1 cup chopped nuts

Heat oven to 350°. Heat margarine and chocolate over low heat, stirring constantly, until melted; cool slightly. Beat sugar, vanilla and eggs in 3-quart bowl on high speed 5 minutes. Beat in chocolate mixture on low speed. Add flour; beat just until blended. Stir in nuts. Spread in greased square pan, 9 × 9 × 2 inches.

Bake just until brownies begin to pull away from sides of pan, 40 to 45 minutes; cool. Cut into about 2-inch squares. 16 brownies.

Marbled Brownies

  Cream Cheese Filling (below)
 1 cup margarine or butter
 4 squares (1 ounce each) unsweetened
   chocolate
 2 cups sugar
 2 teaspoons vanilla
 4 eggs
11/2 cups all-purpose flour
 1/2 teaspoon salt
 1 cup coarsely chopped nuts

Heat oven to 350°. Prepare Cream Cheese Filling. Heat margarine and chocolate over low heat, stirring occasionally, until melted; cool. Beat chocolate mixture, sugar, vanilla and eggs in 2 1/2-quart bowl on medium speed, scraping bowl occasionally, 1 minute. Beat in flour and salt on low speed, scraping bowl occasionally, 30 seconds. Beat on medium speed 1 minute. Stir in nuts.

Spread half of the batter in greased square pan, 9 × 9 × 2 inches; spread with Cream Cheese Filling. Gently spread remaining batter over Cream Cheese Filling. Gently swirl through batter with spoon in an over-and-under motion for marbled effect. Bake until wooden pick inserted in center comes out clean, 55 to 65 minutes; cool. Cut into bars, about 1 1/2 × 1 inch. 48 bars.

Cream Cheese Filling

 1 package (8 ounces) cream cheese, softened
 1/4 cup sugar
 1 teaspoon ground cinnamon
 1 egg
11/2 teaspoons vanilla

Beat all ingredients in 1 1/2-quart bowl, scraping bowl occasionally, 2 minutes.

Frosted Brownies

1/3 cup shortening
2 squares (1 ounce each) unsweetened chocolate
1 cup sugar
1/2 teaspoon vanilla
2 eggs
3/4 cup all-purpose flour
1/2 cup chopped nuts
1/2 teaspoon baking powder
1/2 teaspoon salt
Easy Chocolate Frosting (below)

Heat oven to 350°. Heat shortening and chocolate in 2-quart saucepan over low heat, stirring constantly, until melted. Remove from heat; stir in sugar, vanilla and eggs. Stir in remaining ingredients except frosting. Spread in greased square pan, 8 × 8 × 2 inches.

Bake until brownies begin to pull away from sides of pan, 30 to 35 minutes; cool slightly. Frost with Easy Chocolate Frosting. Cut into about 2-inch squares. 16 brownies.

Easy Chocolate Frosting

1 square (1 ounce) unsweetened chocolate
1 teaspoon margarine or butter
1 cup powdered sugar
1 tablespoon hot water

Heat chocolate and margarine in 1-quart saucepan over low heat, stirring constantly, until melted. Stir in powdered sugar and water; beat until smooth. If necessary, stir in additional hot water, 1 teaspoon at a time, until frosting is of spreading consistency.

Layered Oatmeal Brownies

2 1/2 cups regular or quick-cooking oats
3/4 cup packed brown sugar
3/4 cup all-purpose flour
1/2 teaspoon baking soda
3/4 cup margarine or butter, melted
Brownies (below)

Heat oven to 350°. Mix oats, brown sugar, flour and baking soda; stir in margarine. Reserve 3/4 cup oat mixture. Press remaining mixture in greased rectangular pan, 13 × 9 × 2 inches. Bake 10 minutes; cool 5 minutes.

Prepare Brownies; spread over baked crust. Sprinkle with reserved oat mixture. Bake until brownies begin to pull away from sides of pan, about 35 minutes (do not overbake); cool. Cut into about 1 1/2-inch squares. 48 brownies.

Brownies

2/3 cup shortening
4 squares (1 ounce each) unsweetened chocolate
2 cups sugar
1 teaspoon vanilla
4 eggs
1 1/4 cups all-purpose flour
1 teaspoon baking powder
1 teaspoon salt

Heat shortening and chocolate in 3-quart saucepan over low heat until melted. Remove from heat; mix in sugar, vanilla and eggs. Stir in remaining ingredients.

Marbled Brownies (page 49), Frosted Brownies, Layered Oatmeal Brownies

Caramel Candy Bars

　1　*package (14 ounces) caramel candies*
⅓　*cup milk*
　2　*cups all-purpose flour*
　2　*cups quick-cooking or regular oats*
1½　*cups packed brown sugar*
　1　*teaspoon baking soda*
½　*teaspoon salt*
　1　*egg*
　1　*cup margarine or butter, softened*
　1　*package (6 ounces) semisweet chocolate chips*
　1　*cup chopped walnuts or dry roasted peanuts*

Heat oven to 350°. Heat candies and milk in 2-quart saucepan over low heat, stirring frequently, until smooth.

Mix flour, oats, brown sugar, baking soda, salt and egg. Stir in margarine with fork until mixture is crumbly. Press half of the crumbly mixture in greased rectangular pan, 13 × 9 × 2 inches. Bake 10 minutes. Sprinkle with chocolate chips and walnuts; drizzle with caramel mixture. Sprinkle remaining crumbly mixture over top. Bake until golden brown, 20 to 25 minutes. Cool 30 minutes. Loosen edges from sides of pan; cool completely. Cut into bars, about 2 × 1 inch. 54 bars.

Raisin-Peanut Bars

1　*cup sugar*
1　*cup margarine or butter, softened*
¼　*cup molasses*
1　*teaspoon vanilla*
1　*egg yolk*
2　*cups all-purpose flour*
1　*cup raisins*
1　*cup salted peanuts*
⅓　*cup creamy peanut butter*
1　*package (12 ounces) semisweet chocolate chips*

Heat oven to 350°. Mix sugar, margarine, molasses, vanilla and egg yolk in 2½-quart bowl. Stir in flour. Press dough in ungreased rectangular pan, 13 × 9 × 2 inches. Bake until golden brown, 20 to 25 minutes.

Mix raisins, peanuts, peanut butter and chocolate chips in 2-quart saucepan. Heat over medium-low heat, stirring constantly, until chocolate chips are melted. Spread over crust in pan. Refrigerate at least 2 hours. Cut into bars, about 2 × 1 inch. 54 bars.

Caramel Candy Bars, Raisin-Peanut Bars

Almond Meringue Bars

½ cup granulated sugar
½ cup packed brown sugar
¾ cup margarine or butter, softened
3 eggs, separated
1 teaspoon vanilla
2 cups all-purpose flour
1 teaspoon baking powder
¼ teaspoon baking soda
¼ teaspoon salt
1 package (6 ounces) semisweet chocolate chips
1 cup flaked or shredded coconut
½ cup chopped almonds
1 cup packed brown sugar
½ cup chopped almonds

Heat oven to 350°. Beat granulated sugar, ½ cup brown sugar, the margarine, egg yolks and vanilla in 2½-quart bowl on low speed until blended. Beat on medium speed, scraping bowl constantly, until smooth, about 2 minutes. Stir in flour, baking powder, baking soda and salt. Press dough in greased rectangular pan, 13 × 9 × 2 inches, with floured hands; sprinkle with chocolate chips, coconut and ½ cup almonds.

Beat egg whites until foamy. Beat in 1 cup brown sugar, 1 tablespoon at a time; continue beating until stiff and glossy. Spread over mixture in pan; sprinkle with ½ cup almonds. Bake until meringue is set and light brown, 35 to 40 minutes; cool. Cut into bars, about 3 × 1 inch. 36 bars.

Fruit Bars

1¼ cups all-purpose flour
1 cup sugar
1½ teaspoons baking powder
1 teaspoon salt
½ teaspoon almond extract
3 eggs
1 cup chopped nuts
1 cup cut-up dates or whole raisins
½ cup chopped maraschino cherries, drained
1 package (6 ounces) semisweet chocolate chips

Heat oven to 350°. Mix flour, sugar, baking powder, salt, almond extract and eggs. Stir in remaining ingredients. Spread dough in greased rectangular pan, 13 × 9 × 2 inches.

Bake until light brown, 30 to 35 minutes; cool. Drizzle with Powdered Sugar Frosting (page 54) if desired. Cut into bars, about 2 × 1¼ inches. 36 bars.

Almond Meringue Bars, Fruit Bars

Bonbon Cookies

¾ cup powdered sugar
½ cup margarine or butter, softened
1 tablespoon vanilla
1 square (1 ounce) unsweetened chocolate,
  melted
1½ cups all-purpose flour
⅛ teaspoon salt
  Dates, nuts, semisweet chocolate chips and
    candied or maraschino cherries
  Powdered Sugar Frosting or Chocolate Chip
    Frosting (below)

Heat oven to 350°. Mix powdered sugar, margarine, vanilla and chocolate. Work in flour and salt until dough holds together. (If dough is dry, mix in 1 to 2 tablespoons milk).

Mold dough by tablespoonfuls around date, nut, chocolate chips or cherry. Place cookies about 1 inch apart on ungreased cookie sheet. Bake until set but not brown, 12 to 15 minutes; cool. Dip tops of cookies into Powdered Sugar Frosting. Decorate each with coconut, nuts, colored sugar, chocolate chips or chocolate shot if desired. 20 to 25 cookies.

Powdered Sugar Frosting

Mix 1 cup powdered sugar, 1 tablespoon plus 1½ teaspoons milk and 1 teaspoon vanilla. If desired, stir in few drops food color.

Chocolate Chip Frosting

½ cup semisweet chocolate chips
2 tablespoons margarine or butter
2 tablespoons water
½ cup powdered sugar

Heat chocolate chips, margarine and water over low heat, stirring constantly, until melted. Remove from heat; stir in powdered sugar until smooth.

Apricot Thumbprint Cookies

½ cup packed brown sugar
½ cup shortening
3 tablespoons cocoa
½ teaspoon vanilla
1 egg
1 cup all-purpose flour
¼ teaspoon salt
  Apricot preserves or jam
  Chocolate Chip Glaze (below)

Heat oven to 350°. Mix brown sugar, shortening, cocoa, vanilla and egg in 2½-quart bowl; stir in flour and salt. Shape dough by measuring tablespoonfuls into balls. Place on ungreased cookie sheet 3 inches apart; press thumb deeply in center of each. Bake until firm, 8 to 10 minutes.

Immediately remove from cookie sheet; cool. Fill thumbprints with apricot preserves. Spread with Chocolate Chip Glaze. About 2 dozen cookies.

Chocolate Chip Glaze

Heat ½ cup semisweet chocolate chips, 2 tablespoons margarine or butter and 1 tablespoon corn syrup over low heat, stirring constantly, until chocolate is melted; cool slightly.

COCONUT THUMBPRINT COOKIES: Omit apricot preserves. Mix 1 cup flaked coconut, ¼ cup powdered sugar and 2 tablespoons margarine or butter, softened. Fill thumbprints with coconut mixture. Top each with whole almond if desired. Spread with Chocolate Chip Glaze.

Peanut Butter-filled Pretzels

¾ cup powdered sugar
½ cup margarine or butter, softened
1 teaspoon vanilla
1 egg
1½ cups all-purpose flour
¼ cup cocoa
½ teaspoon baking soda
½ teaspoon cream of tartar
    Peanut Butter Filling (right)
    Cocoa Glaze (right)

Mix powdered sugar and margarine in 2½-quart bowl; stir in vanilla and egg. Stir in flour, cocoa, baking soda and cream of tartar. Refrigerate until chilled, 2 to 3 hours.

Heat oven to 375°. Prepare Peanut Butter Filling. Divide dough into halves. Roll each into rectangle, about 13½×9 inches, on well-floured cloth-covered board. Cut each crosswise into nine 1½-inch strips. Shape Peanut Butter Filling into eighteen 1¼-inch balls. Roll each ball into rope, 9 inches long, on floured surface. Place ropes on centers of chocolate strips. Bring long edges of each strip up over filling; seal well. Shape into pretzel on ungreased cookie sheet. Bake until set, 8 to 10 minutes; cool. Spread with Cocoa Glaze; sprinkle with chopped peanuts if desired. 1½ dozen cookies.

Peanut Butter Filling

Mix ¾ cup creamy peanut butter and 3 tablespoons margarine or butter, softened. Gradually stir in 1 cup powdered sugar.

Cocoa Glaze

Mix 1 cup powdered sugar and 2 tablespoons cocoa. Stir in 2 tablespoons milk until smooth. If necessary, stir in additional milk, ½ teaspoon at a time, until of desired consistency.

PEANUT BUTTER-FILLED LOGS: Do not shape into pretzels. Cut each 9-inch peanut butter-filled chocolate strip into three 3-inch pieces. Bake on ungreased cookie sheet 7 to 8 minutes. 4½ dozen cookies.

PEANUT BUTTER-FILLED ROUNDS: Pat or roll each half dough into rectangle, 15×3 inches. Divide Peanut Butter Filling into halves. Shape each half into rope, 15 inches long. Place ropes on centers of rectangles. Bring long edges up over filling; seal well. Cut into ½-inch slices. (If desired, slices can be flattened with bottom of glass dipped in sugar.) Bake on ungreased cookie sheet 7 to 8 minutes. Omit Cocoa Glaze. 5 dozen cookies.

Peanut Butter-filled Pretzels

Pinwheels

Slice 'n Easy Cookies

1 cup granulated sugar
1 cup packed brown sugar
⅔ cup shortening
⅔ cup margarine or butter, softened
2 teaspoons vanilla
2 eggs
3¼ cups all-purpose flour
½ cup cocoa
1 teaspoon baking soda
1 teaspoon salt

Mix sugars, shortening, margarine, vanilla and eggs in 4-quart bowl. Stir in remaining ingredients. Turn dough onto lightly floured surface. Shape into ball with lightly floured hands, pressing to make dough compact. Cut dough into halves. Shape each half into roll, about 2 inches in diameter and about 8 inches long. Wrap and refrigerate at least 8 hours before slicing. (Roll can be refrigerated no longer than 1 month or frozen no longer than 3 months.)

Heat oven to 375°. Cut roll into ¼-inch slices. (It is not necessary to thaw frozen roll before slicing.) Place slices about 2 inches apart on ungreased cookie sheet. Bake until set, 6 to 8 minutes. Immediately remove from cookie sheet onto wire rack. About 5½ dozen cookies.

CHOCOLATE CHIP COOKIES: Omit cocoa. Stir in 1 cup miniature semisweet chocolate chips and 1 cup chopped nuts with the flour.

NUT COOKIES: Stir in 1 cup chopped nuts with the flour.

MINT SANDWICH COOKIES: Cut roll into ⅛-inch slices. Bake until set, about 6 minutes. Mix 4 cups powdered sugar, ½ cup margarine or butter, softened, and 1 teaspoon mint extract. Stir in 3 to 4 tablespoons water until smooth and of spreading consistency. Tint with few drops green or red food color if desired. Put cooled cookies together in pairs with powdered sugar mixture.

PINWHEELS: Omit cocoa. Divide dough into fourths. Roll each fourth into rectangle, 10 × 8 inches, on lightly floured waxed paper. Prepare Fudge Filling (below); spread over each rectangle. Roll up tightly, beginning at 10-inch side. Pinch edge of dough into roll to seal. Refrigerate roll at least 8 hours before slicing. Bake cookies on lightly greased cookie sheet. About 13 dozen cookies.

Fudge Filling

Heat 1½ cups semisweet chocolate chips and ¼ cup margarine or butter in 1-quart saucepan over low heat, stirring constantly, until melted. Remove from heat; stir in ½ cup finely chopped nuts and 2 tablespoons all-purpose flour; cool slightly.

Chocolate Cookie Dough

1 cup sugar
½ cup margarine or butter, softened
⅓ cup milk
1 teaspoon vanilla
1 egg
2 envelopes (1 ounce each) premelted chocolate
2 cups all-purpose flour
1 cup chopped pecans
½ teaspoon baking powder
½ teaspoon salt

Mix sugar, margarine, milk, vanilla, egg and chocolate in 2½-quart bowl. Mix in remaining ingredients on low speed, scraping bowl constantly, until soft dough forms.

Caramel Cookies

½ Chocolate Cookie Dough (above)
18 caramel candies or candied cherries, cut into halves
1½ cups powdered sugar
1 envelope (1 ounce) premelted chocolate
2 tablespoons light corn syrup
2 to 3 tablespoons hot water

Refrigerate dough 1 to 2 hours for easier handling. Heat oven to 400°. Mold dough by rounded teaspoonfuls around candy halves; place on ungreased cookie sheet. Bake until set, about 7 minutes; cool. Mix powdered sugar, chocolate, corn syrup and water until smooth. Swirl cookies in chocolate glaze. About 3 dozen cookies.

Coconut Balls

2 cups flaked coconut
½ Chocolate Cookie Dough (above)

Heat oven to 400°. Work coconut into dough. Shape dough by rounded teaspoonfuls into balls. If desired, roll balls in additional coconut; place on ungreased cookie sheet. Bake until set, about 7 minutes. 4 dozen cookies.

Crème de Menthe Cookies

⅔ cup margarine or butter, softened
½ cup granulated sugar
1 egg
2 cups all-purpose flour
½ teaspoon salt
2 cups powdered sugar
3 tablespoons green crème de menthe
About 2 tablespoons milk
2 squares (1 ounce each) unsweetened chocolate
¼ teaspoon shortening

Mix margarine, granulated sugar and egg. Stir in flour and salt. Cover and refrigerate until chilled, about 1 hour.

Heat oven to 325°. Shape dough by rounded teaspoonfuls into balls. Place balls on ungreased cookie sheet; flatten with bottom of glass dipped in granulated sugar. Bake just until set but not brown, 8 to 10 minutes. Immediately remove from cookie sheet; cool.

Beat powdered sugar, crème de menthe and milk in small bowl until smooth. If necessary, stir in additional milk, ½ teaspoon at a time, until of spreading consistency. Spread over top of cookies. Heat chocolate and shortening in 1-quart saucepan over low heat, stirring constantly, until melted. Drizzle chocolate frosting over green frosting. Let frosted cookies stand at least 8 hours before storing. Store cookies loosely covered. About 4½ dozen cookies.

Desserts

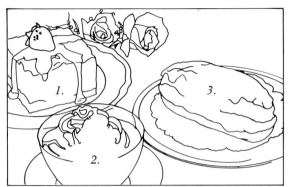

1. Fudgy Meringue Mallow, 2. Chocolate Mousse, 3. Chocolate Cheese Eclair

Chocolate Cream Pudding

½ cup sugar
⅓ cup cocoa
2 tablespoons cornstarch
⅛ teaspoon salt
2 cups milk
2 egg yolks, slightly beaten
2 tablespoons margarine or butter, softened
2 teaspoons vanilla

Mix sugar, cocoa, cornstarch and salt in 2-quart saucepan. Stir in milk gradually. Cook over medium heat, stirring constantly, until mixture thickens and boils. Boil and stir 1 minute. Stir at least half of the hot mixture gradually into egg yolks. Blend into hot mixture in saucepan. Boil and stir 1 minute. Remove from heat; stir in margarine and vanilla. Pour into dessert dishes. Cool slightly; refrigerate. 4 servings.

Hot Fudge Sundae Cake

1 cup all-purpose flour
¾ cup granulated sugar
2 tablespoons cocoa
2 teaspoons baking powder
¼ teaspoon salt
½ cup milk
2 tablespoons salad oil
1 teaspoon vanilla
1 cup chopped nuts, if desired
1 cup packed brown sugar
¼ cup cocoa
1¾ cups hottest tap water
Ice Cream

Heat oven to 350°. In ungreased square pan, 9 × 9 × 2 inches, stir together flour, granulated sugar, 2 tablespoons cocoa, the baking powder and salt. Mix in milk, oil and vanilla with fork until smooth. Stir in nuts. Spread evenly in pan. Sprinkle with brown sugar and ¼ cup cocoa. Pour hot water over batter.

Bake 40 minutes. Let stand 15 minutes; spoon into dessert dishes or cut into squares. Invert each square onto dessert plate. Top with ice cream and spoon some of the remaining sauce over each serving. 9 servings.

BUTTERSCOTCH SUNDAE CAKE: Substitute 1 package (6 ounces) butterscotch chips (1 cup) for the nuts. Decrease brown sugar to ½ cup and the ¼ cup cocoa to 2 tablespoons.

COCONUT SUNDAE CAKE: Substitute ½ cup shredded coconut and ½ cup chopped almonds for the nuts.

MALLOW SUNDAE CAKE: Substitute 1 cup miniature marshmallows for the nuts.

PEANUTTY SUNDAE CAKE: Substitute ½ cup peanut butter and ½ cup chopped peanuts for the nuts.

RAISIN SUNDAE CAKE: Substitute 1 cup raisins for the nuts.

Pink Peppermint Cups

  8 to 10 *Chocolate Crepes (page 73)*
24 *large marshmallows or 2 cups miniature*
       marshmallows
½ *cup milk*
  1 *teaspoon vanilla*
⅛ *teaspoon salt*
⅛ *teaspoon peppermint extract*
  3 to 5 *drops red food coloring*
  1 *cup chilled whipping cream*
  2 *tablespoons crushed peppermint stick candy*

Place each crepe, prettiest side down, on 6- to 8-inch square of heavy-duty aluminum foil, depending on size of crepe. Trim foil to make circles the same size as the crepes. Shape foil and crepe together to form cup by turning up 1½- to 2-inch edge; flute. Place on ungreased cookie sheet. Bake in 350° oven until crisp, about 15 minutes. Cool and remove foil.

Heat marshmallows and milk in 3-quart saucepan over medium heat, stirring constantly, *just* until marshmallows are melted. Remove from heat; stir in vanilla, salt, extract and food coloring. Place pan in bowl of ice and water or refrigerate, stirring occasionally, until mixture mounds slightly when dropped from a spoon.

Beat whipping cream in chilled bowl until stiff. Stir marshmallow mixture until blended; fold in whipped cream. Spoon into crepe cups. Refrigerate until set, at least 3 hours. Just before serving, sprinkle with crushed candy. 8 to 10 servings.

NOTE: Crepe Cups can also be filled with peppermint or vanilla ice cream, cut-up fresh fruit or Chocolate Mousse (page 63).

Pink Peppermint Cups

Pink Peppermint Cups

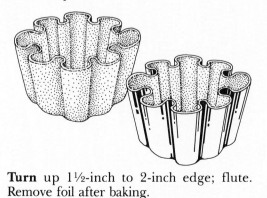

Trim aluminum foil to make circles the same size as crepes.

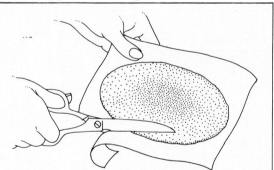

Turn up 1½-inch to 2-inch edge; flute. Remove foil after baking.

Fruit and Pudding Parfaits

*1 package (about 4½ ounces) instant chocolate
    flavor pudding and pie filling*
1 cup milk
1 cup chilled whipping cream
*½ teaspoon almond extract or ½ teaspoon
    ground cinnamon*
½ cup chilled whipping cream, if desired
1 to 1½ cups sliced fresh fruit

Beat pudding and milk in 1½-quart bowl on low speed until smooth. Add 1 cup whipping cream and the extract; beat on medium speed until soft peaks form, 2 to 3 minutes. Beat ½ cup whipping cream in chilled bowl until stiff.

Alternate layers of fruit, pudding and whipped cream, in parfait glasses or dessert dishes. Refrigerate at least 15 minutes. Garnish with sliced fruit and mint leaves, toasted flaked coconut or chopped nuts if desired. 6 servings.

NOTE: If using banana or pear slices for garnish, dip the slices into lemon juice to prevent discoloration.

APRICOT AND PUDDING PARFAITS: Substitute 1 tablespoon plus 1 teaspoon apricot brandy for the almond extract; use sliced fresh apricots.

ORANGE AND PUDDING PARFAITS: Substitute 1 tablespoon plus 1 teaspoon orange-flavored liqueur for the almond extract; use cut-up fresh oranges.

PEAR AND PUDDING PARFAITS: Substitute ¼ teaspoon ground nutmeg for the almond extract; use sliced fresh pears.

Apricot and Pudding Parfaits

Cinnamon Custard

1/4 cup chocolate fudge ice-cream topping
3 eggs, slightly beaten
1/3 cup sugar
1 teaspoon ground cinnamon
1 teaspoon vanilla
    Dash of salt
2 1/2 cups milk, scalded

Heat oven to 350°. Spoon 2 teaspoons of the topping into each of six 6-ounce custard cups. Mix remaining ingredients except milk in 2 1/2-quart bowl. Stir in milk gradually. Pour into custard cups. Place cups in rectangular pan, 13 × 9 × 2 inches, on oven rack. Pour very hot water into pan to within 1/2 inch of tops of cups.

Bake until knife inserted halfway between center and edge comes out clean, about 45 minutes. Remove cups from water; refrigerate at least 1 hour. Unmold on dessert plates. Refrigerate any remaining custard no longer than 48 hours. 6 servings.

Mocha Cream Pudding

1 package (about 3 1/2 ounces) regular chocolate
    pudding mix
2 teaspoons instant coffee
2 cups milk
1 cup chilled whipping cream

Mix pudding and coffee in saucepan. Slowly add milk, stirring to keep mixture smooth. Cook over medium heat, stirring constantly, until mixture thickens and boils. Pour into a bowl; place waxed paper directly on pudding. Refrigerate.

Beat whipping cream in chilled bowl until stiff. Beat pudding to soften; fold into whipped cream. Spoon into serving dishes. Refrigerate. Garnish with whipped cream and sprinkle with instant coffee if desired. 6 to 8 servings.

Chocolate Mousse

4 squares (1 ounce each) semisweet chocolate,
    cut into pieces
3 eggs, separated
1 teaspoon vanilla
3/4 teaspoon cream of tartar
1/2 cup sugar
1 cup chilled whipping cream

Heat chocolate in heavy saucepan over low heat, stirring occasionally, until chocolate is melted. Remove from heat. Beat egg yolks slightly; stir yolks and vanilla into melted chocolate. Beat egg whites and cream of tartar in 2 1/2-quart bowl until foamy. Beat in sugar, 1 tablespoon at a time; continue beating until stiff and glossy. Stir about 1/4 of the meringue into chocolate mixture. Fold into remaining meringue.

Beat whipping cream in chilled 1 1/2-quart bowl until stiff. Fold into chocolate mixture. Spoon into dessert dishes. Refrigerate at least 2 hours. Top each serving with additional sweetened whipped cream and grated chocolate or desired chocolate design (see Chocolate Flowers page 24). 8 servings (about 1/2 cup each).

BRANDY CHOCOLATE MOUSSE: Fold in 2 tablespoons brandy with the whipped cream.

WHIPPED CHOCOLATE PUDDING

Beat 1 package (about 4 1/2 ounces) chocolate flavor instant pudding and 1 cup milk in 1 1/2-quart bowl at low speed. Add 2 cups chilled whipping cream; beat at medium speed until soft peaks form, about 2 minutes. Pour into serving dishes. Refrigerate at least 15 to 20 minutes. Garnish with whipped cream and/or grated chocolate if desired. 6 to 8 servings.

Chocolate Terrine

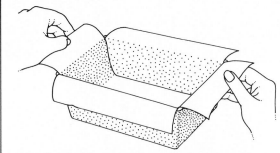

Line loaf pan, 8½ × 4½ × 2½ inches, with two strips of aluminum foil, leaving about 2 inches overhanging sides.

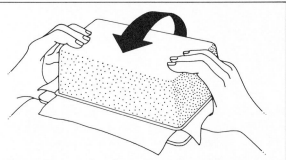

To remove terrine from pan, place oblong serving plate on top of pan, and holding both tightly, invert plate and pan together; remove foil.

Chocolate Terrine

1 package (3½ ounces) almond paste
1½ cups half-and-half
4 squares (1 ounce each) semisweet chocolate, coarsely chopped
4 ounces white chocolate (vanilla-flavored candy coating), coarsely chopped
4 eggs, slightly beaten
2 tablespoons brandy
Chocolate Glaze (right)

Line loaf pan, 8½ × 4½ × 2½ inches, with aluminum foil, leaving about 2 inches overhanging sides. Roll almond paste between 2 sheets waxed paper into rectangle, 8 × 4 inches; cover with plastic wrap and set aside.

Heat oven to 350°. Heat half-and-half, semisweet chocolate and white chocolate over low heat, stirring constantly, until chocolates are melted and mixture is smooth; cool slightly. Gradually stir eggs and brandy into chocolate mixture. Pour into lined pan.

Place pan in pan of very hot water (1 inch deep) in oven. Bake until knife inserted halfway between edge and center comes out clean, 40 to 50 minutes. Remove from water. Remove waxed paper from almond paste and immediately place on hot terrine; cool 1 hour. Cover and refrigerate at least 6 hours but no longer than 24 hours.

Prepare Chocolate Glaze; reserve ¼ cup. Remove terrine from pan by inverting on serving plate. Carefully remove foil. Spread remaining glaze evenly and smoothly over sides and top of terrine.

Stir 1 to 2 tablespoons powdered sugar into reserved chocolate glaze until smooth and of desired consistency. Place in decorating bag with small writing tip or small sturdy plastic storage bag. (If using plastic bag, cut off very small corner of bag, about ⅛ inch in diameter.) Write "Terrine" on top and decorate around edges of top with remaining chocolate. To serve, cut into 8 slices, about 1 inch each; cut slices into halves. Refrigerate any remaining terrine. 16 servings.

Chocolate Glaze

Heat 1 cup semisweet chocolate chips, ¼ cup margarine or butter and 2 tablespoons corn syrup over low heat, stirring constantly, until chocolate is melted; cool.

Peanut Brittle Bread Pudding

4 cups soft bread cubes (4 to 5 slices bread)
½ cup coarsely broken peanut brittle
½ cup semisweet chocolate chips
1 egg
½ cup milk
½ cup packed brown sugar
¼ cup margarine or butter, melted
1 cup chilled whipping cream
¼ cup chocolate-flavored syrup

Heat oven to 350°. Place 2 cups of the bread cubes in greased 1-quart casserole. Sprinkle with half of the peanut brittle and half of the chocolate chips; repeat with remaining bread cubes, peanut brittle and chocolate chips. Beat egg; stir in milk, brown sugar and margarine. Pour over bread mixture. Bake 30 minutes.

Beat whipping cream and syrup in 1-quart chilled bowl until soft peaks form. Serve with warm pudding. 6 servings.

Fudgy Meringue Mallow

6 egg whites
½ teaspoon cream of tartar
¼ teaspoon salt
1½ cups sugar
⅓ cup cocoa
2 packages (3 ounces each) cream cheese, softened
½ cup sugar
1 teaspoon vanilla
½ teaspoon almond extract
2 cups chilled whipping cream
2 cups miniature marshmallows
Glossy Chocolate Sauce (page 80)

Heat oven to 275°. Grease rectangular pan, 13 × 9 × 2 inches. Beat egg whites, cream of tartar and salt in 2½-quart bowl until foamy. Beat in 1½ cups sugar, 1 tablespoon at a time; beat until stiff and glossy. Do not underbeat. Beat in cocoa on low speed just until mixed. Spread evenly in pan. Bake 1 hour. Turn off oven; leave in oven with door closed at least 12 hours.

Mix cream cheese, ½ cup sugar, the vanilla and almond extract. Beat whipping cream in chilled 2½-quart bowl until stiff. Fold cream cheese mixture and marshmallows into whipped cream. Spread over meringue; refrigerate at least 12 hours. Cut into serving pieces; serve with Glossy Chocolate Sauce. Garnish each serving with a whole strawberry if desired. 10 to 12 servings.

Chocolate Soufflé

⅓ cup sugar
⅓ cup cocoa
¼ cup all-purpose flour
1 cup milk
3 egg yolks
2 tablespoons margarine or butter, softened
1 teaspoon vanilla
4 egg whites
¼ teaspoon cream of tartar
⅛ teaspoon salt
3 tablespoons sugar
Creamy Sauce (below)

Mix ⅓ cup sugar, the cocoa and flour in 1-quart saucepan. Stir in milk gradually. Heat, stirring constantly, until mixture boils. Remove from heat. Beat yolks in 1½-quart bowl with fork. Beat in about ⅓ of cocoa mixture. Stir in remaining cocoa mixture gradually. Stir in butter and vanilla. Cool slightly.

Place oven rack in lowest position. Heat oven to 350°. Butter and sugar 6-cup soufflé dish. Make 4-inch band of triple thickness aluminum foil 2 inches longer than circumference of dish. Butter and sugar one side of foil band. Extend height of soufflé dish 2 inches by securing foil band buttered side in around outside edge of dish.

Beat egg whites, cream of tartar and salt in 2½-quart bowl until foamy. Beat in 3 tablespoons sugar, 1 tablespoon at a time; continue beating until stiff and glossy. Do not underbeat. Stir about ¼ of the egg whites into chocolate mixture. Fold in remaining whites. Pour carefully into soufflé dish. Place dish in square pan, 9 × 9 × 2 inches, on oven rack; pour very hot water (1 inch deep) into pan. Bake 1¼ hours. Serve immediately with Creamy Sauce. 6 servings.

Creamy Sauce

Heat ½ cup powdered sugar, ½ cup margarine or butter and ½ cup whipping cream to boiling in 1-quart saucepan over medium heat, stirring occasionally.

Pots de Crème

Pots de Crème

1½ cups semisweet chocolate chips
2 cups half-and-half
4 eggs
¼ cup granulated sugar
¼ teaspoon salt
½ cup chilled whipping cream
1 tablespoon powdered sugar

Heat oven to 350°. Heat chocolate chips and half-and-half over medium heat, stirring constantly, until chocolate is melted and mixture is smooth. Cool slightly. Beat eggs, granulated sugar and salt; stir into chocolate mixture gradually. Pour into 8 to 10 ovenproof pots de crème cups, or 8 ramekins or 6-ounce custard cups.

Place cups in baking pan, 13 × 9 × 2 inches, on oven rack. Pour boiling water into pan to within ½ inch of tops of cups. Bake 20 minutes. Cool slightly. Cover and refrigerate at least 4 hours but no longer than 24 hours.

Beat whipping cream and powdered sugar in chilled bowl until stiff. Top with sweetened whipped cream and, if desired, candy mints, cut diagonally into halves. 8 to 10 servings.

MOCHA POTS DE CRÈME: Beat in 1 to 1½ teaspoons instant coffee with eggs, sugar and salt.

MINT POTS DE CRÈME: Decrease half-and-half to 1¾ cups; stir ¼ cup crème de menthe into chocolate mixture after cooling. Pour 1 teaspoon crème de menthe over whipped cream on each serving.

Chocolate Cheesecake

*1¼ cups chocolate wafer crumbs or graham
      cracker crumbs (about 20 wafers or 16
      squares)*
2 tablespoons sugar
3 tablespoons margarine or butter, melted
1 package (6 ounces) semisweet chocolate chips
*2 packages (8 ounces each) cream cheese,
      softened*
2 teaspoons vanilla
1 cup sugar
3 eggs
1 cup dairy sour cream
      Sour Cream Topping (below)

Mix wafer crumbs, 2 tablespoons sugar and
the margarine. Press in bottom of springform
pan, 9 × 3 inches.

Heat oven to 300°. Heat chocolate chips over
low heat, stirring occasionally, until melted;
cool slightly. Beat cream cheese and vanilla in
2½-quart bowl until smooth. Add 1 cup sugar
gradually, beating until fluffy. Beat in eggs,
one at a time. Beat in chocolate and sour
cream until smooth. Pour into pan.

Bake until center is firm, 65 to 70 minutes;
cool to room temperature. Refrigerate at least
3 hours but no longer than 10 days. Loosen
edge of cheesecake with knife before removing side of pan. Spread with topping. Sprinkle
with chopped or grated chocolate if desired.
Refrigerate any remaining cheesecake. 12
servings.

Sour Cream Topping

Mix 1 cup dairy sour cream, 2 tablespoons
sugar and 2 teaspoons vanilla.

Marble Cheesecake

*1¼ cups chocolate wafer crumbs (about 20
      wafers)*
2 tablespoons sugar
3 tablespoons margarine or butter, melted
1 package (6 ounces) semisweet chocolate chips
*2 packages (8 ounces each) plus 1 package
      (3 ounces) cream cheese, softened*
¼ teaspoon vanilla
1 cup sugar
3 eggs
1 cup dairy sour cream, if desired

Mix wafer crumbs, 2 tablespoons sugar and
the margarine. Press in bottom of springform
pan, 9 × 3 inches.

Heat oven to 300°. Heat chocolate chips over
low heat, stirring occasionally, until melted;
cool slightly. Beat cream cheese and vanilla in
3-quart bowl until smooth. Add 1 cup sugar
gradually, beating until fluffy. Beat in eggs,
one at a time. Divide batter into halves. Stir
chocolate into 1 half. Spoon batters alternately
into pan. Cut through batters with knife or
spatula several times for marbled effect.

Bake until center is firm, 55 to 65 minutes;
cool to room temperature. Refrigerate at least
3 hours but no longer than 10 days. Loosen
edge of cheesecake with knife before removing side of pan. Spread top of cheesecake with
sour cream. Refrigerate any remaining
cheesecake. 12 servings.

Marble Cheesecake, Chocolate Cheesecake

Brownie Torte

Brownie Torte

    1 package (15.5 ounces) fudge brownie mix
    1/4 cup water
    1/4 cup vegetable oil
    2 eggs
    1/2 cup finely chopped nuts
    1 1/2 cups chilled whipping cream or 3 cups
         frozen whipped topping*
    1/3 cup packed brown sugar
    1 tablespoon instant coffee
         Shaved chocolate

Heat oven to 350°. Grease and flour 2 round pans, 9 × 1 1/2 inches. Blend brownie mix (dry), water, oil and eggs. Stir in nuts. Spread in pans. Bake 18 to 20 minutes. Remove from pans. Cool completely on wire racks.

Beat whipping cream in chilled bowl until it begins to thicken. Gradually add sugar and coffee; continue beating until stiff. Fill layers with 1 cup of the whipped cream mixture. Sprinkle with chocolate. Refrigerate at least 1 hour. 10 to 12 servings.

*If using frozen whipped topping, thaw and omit the brown sugar.

Brownie Mint Dessert

    1 package (21.5 ounces) fudge brownie mix
    1/3 cup plus 1 tablespoon water
    2 tablespoons vegetable oil
    1 egg
         Mint Topping (below)

Heat oven to 350°. Grease bottom only of rectangular pan, 13 × 9 × 2 inches. Mix all ingredients except Mint Topping. Spread in pan. Bake 23 to 27 minutes; cool. Spread with Mint Topping. Garnish with grated semisweet chocolate if desired. Refrigerate at least 4 hours. 15 servings.

Mint Topping

    32 large marshmallows
    1/2 cup milk
    1 1/2 cups chilled whipping cream
    2 tablespoons green crème de menthe
    1 tablespoon white crème de cacao
         Few drops green food color, if desired

Heat marshmallows and milk in 2-quart saucepan over low heat, stirring constantly, until marshmallows are melted. Refrigerate until thickened, stirring occasionally. Beat whipping cream in chilled bowl until stiff. Stir marshmallow mixture until blended; stir in liqueurs. Fold marshmallow mixture into whipped cream. Fold in food color.

Mocha Meringue Torte

4 egg whites
½ teaspoon cream of tartar
1 cup sugar
Mocha Filling (right)

Heat oven to 275°. Cover 2 cookie sheets with brown paper. Beat egg whites and cream of tartar in 2½-quart bowl until foamy. Beat in sugar, 1 tablespoon at a time; continue beating until stiff and glossy. Do not underbeat.

Divide meringue into 3 parts. Place 1 part on 1 cookie sheet; shape into 6-inch circle. Shape two 6-inch circles on second cookie sheet. Bake 45 minutes. Turn off oven; leave meringue in oven with door closed 1 hour. Remove meringue from oven.

Fill layers and frost top of torte with Mocha Filling. Torte will be easier to cut if frozen. Decorate with Chocolate Curls (page 27) if desired. To cut, dip knife in hot water and wipe after cutting each slice.

Mocha Filling

2 packages (about 1.4 ounces each) dessert
   topping mix
¼ cup sugar
3 tablespoons cocoa
1 or 2 tablespoons instant coffee

Prepare dessert topping mix as directed on package except — before beating, add sugar, cocoa and instant coffee.

Mocha Meringue Torte

Chocolate Cherry Puffs

Chocolate Cherry Puffs

¾ cup plus 2 tablespoons all-purpose flour
2 tablespoons cocoa
1 tablespoon sugar
½ cup margarine or butter
1 cup water
4 eggs
   Cream Filling (right)
1 can (21 ounces) cherry pie filling
   Powdered sugar

Heat oven to 400°. Mix flour, cocoa and sugar. Heat margarine and water to a rolling boil in 2-quart saucepan. Stir in flour mixture. Stir vigorously over low heat until mixture forms a ball, about 1 minute. Remove from heat. Beat in eggs, all at once; continue beating until smooth. Drop dough by about ¼ cupfuls 3 inches apart onto ungreased cookie sheet. Bake until puffed and darker brown on top, 35 to 40 minutes; cool.

Cut off tops; pull out any filaments of soft dough. Fill puffs with Cream Filling and cher-ry pie filling. Replace tops; dust with pow-dered sugar. Serve with chocolate sauce if de-sired. 8 to 10 servings.

Cream Filling

1 cup dairy sour cream or unflavored yogurt
1 cup milk
1 package (about 3½ ounces) vanilla instant
   pudding and pie filling mix

Beat sour cream and milk with hand beater in a 2½-quart bowl until smooth. Beat in instant pudding until smooth and slightly thickened, about 2 minutes.

ICE CREAM PUFFS: Fill puffs with peppermint, coffee or vanilla ice cream.

FRUIT CREAM PUFFS: Beat ¾ cup chilled whip-ping cream and ¾ cup sugar in chilled bowl until stiff. Fold in ¾ cup cut-up fresh fruit (strawberries, bananas, apricots, raspberries or cherries). Fill puffs.

Chocolate Cheese Eclairs

¾ cup plus 2 tablespoons all-purpose flour
2 tablespoons cocoa
1 tablespoon sugar
1 cup water
½ cup margarine or butter
4 eggs
  Chocolate Cheese Filling (below)
  Cocoa Glaze (page 55)

Heat oven to 400°. Mix flour, cocoa and sugar. Heat water and margarine in 3-quart saucepan to a rolling boil. Stir in flour mixture. Stir vigorously over low heat until mixture forms a ball, about 1 minute. Remove from heat. Beat in eggs; continue beating until smooth. Drop dough by about ¼ cupfuls 3 inches apart onto ungreased cookie sheet. With spatula, shape each into finger 4½ inches long and 1½ inches wide. Bake until puffed and darker brown on top, 35 to 40 minutes; cool.

Cut off tops; pull out any filaments of soft dough. Fill eclairs with Chocolate Cheese Filling; replace tops. Spread with Cocoa Glaze just before serving. Refrigerate any remaining eclairs. 8 to 10 eclairs.

Chocolate Cheese Filling

¼ cup semisweet chocolate chips
1 package (3 ounces) cream cheese, softened
⅓ cup packed brown sugar
¼ cup milk
½ teaspoon vanilla
1 cup chilled whipping cream

Heat chocolate chips in small heavy saucepan over low heat, stirring occasionally, until melted; cool. Beat cream cheese, brown sugar, milk and vanilla until smooth and creamy. Stir in chocolate. Beat whipping cream in chilled bowl until soft peaks form. Fold in chocolate mixture.

Ginger Cream Crepes

Chocolate Crepes (below)
2 cups chilled whipping cream
½ cup packed brown sugar
⅓ cup finely chopped crystallized ginger
  Powdered sugar

Prepare Chocolate Crepes. Beat whipping cream and brown sugar in chilled 2½-quart bowl until stiff. Fold in ginger. Spoon about ¼ cup of the whipped cream mixture onto each crepe; roll up. Place 2 crepes, seam sides down, on each dessert plate; sprinkle with powdered sugar. Serve with chocolate sauce if desired. 8 servings (2 crepes each).

Chocolate Crepes

1¼ cups all-purpose flour
3 tablespoons cocoa
2 tablespoons sugar
½ teaspoon baking powder
½ teaspoon salt
2 cups milk
2 tablespoons margarine or butter, melted
½ teaspoon vanilla
2 eggs

Mix flour, cocoa, sugar, baking powder and salt. Stir in remaining ingredients. Beat with hand beater until smooth. Generously butter 6- to 8-inch skillet; heat over medium heat until bubbly. For each crepe, pour scant ¼ cup of the batter into skillet; *immediately* rotate skillet until thin film covers bottom.

Cook until crepe surface begins to dry. Run spatula around edge to loosen; turn and cook other side until light brown. Stack crepes, placing waxed paper between each. Keep covered.

DO-AHEAD CREPES

Make crepes ahead, then refrigerate or freeze them. Stack 6 to 8 together, with a layer of waxed paper between each. Wrap and refrigerate for several days. For long-term storage, wrap, label (with date) and freeze. When ready to use, thaw (wrapped) at room temperature about 3 hours.

Chocolate-dipped Strawberries

9 to 12 large strawberries with leaves
1 package (6 ounces) semisweet chocolate chips, melted

Cover each strawberry ¾ of the way with melted chocolate (top of strawberry and leaves should be visible); place on waxed paper. Refrigerate uncovered until chocolate is firm, about 30 minutes. 3 or 4 servings.

STRAWBERRIES ON CREAM: Beat ½ cup chilled whipping cream and 1 tablespoon cherry or apricot brandy in chilled 1½-quart bowl until stiff. Divide whipped cream among 4 dishes; top each with 3 chocolate-dipped strawberries. 4 servings.

Banana Shortcake

1⅓ cups buttermilk baking mix
½ cup sugar
⅓ cup cocoa
⅔ cup milk
3 tablespoons margarine or butter, softened
1 egg
1 pint vanilla ice cream or sweetened whipped cream
1 banana, sliced

Heat oven to 350°. Grease and flour square pan, 8×8×2 inches. Beat all ingredients except ice cream and banana on low speed, scraping bowl frequently, 30 seconds. Beat on medium speed, 4 minutes. Pour into pan.

Bake until wooden pick inserted in center comes out clean, 35 to 40 minutes. Serve warm topped with ice cream and banana slices and, if desired, chocolate sauce. 8 or 9 servings.

SPICED BANANA SHORTCAKE: Add 1 teaspoon ground cinnamon before beating.

Chocolate Fondue

12 ounces milk chocolate, semisweet chocolate chips or sweet cooking chocolate
½ cup half-and-half
1 to 3 tablespoons orange-flavored liqueur, kirsch, brandy, white crème de menthe or 2 teaspoons instant coffee (dry) or ¼ teaspoon ground cinnamon
Dippers (below)

Heat chocolate and half-and-half in heavy saucepan over low heat, stirring constantly, until chocolate is melted and mixture is smooth. Remove from heat; stir in liqueur. Pour into fondue pot or chafing dish with water bath; keep warm over very low heat.

Guests select choice of Dippers and place on dessert plates; then, with fondue forks or bamboo skewers, they dip each one into chocolate mixture. If mixture becomes too thick, stir in small amount of cream. Dippers can be rolled in granola, chopped peanuts, chopped salted cashews or cookie coconut after coating with chocolate mixture if desired. 6 to 8 servings.

Dippers

Strawberries	*Kiwifruit slices*
*Banana slices**	*Fresh coconut chunks*
Pineapple chunks	*Pound cake cubes*
Mandarin orange segments	*Ladyfingers*
Fresh orange slices	*Miniature cream puffs*
*Apple wedges**	*Miniature doughnuts*
Grapes	*Marshmallows*
Melon balls	*Pretzels*
*Papaya wedges**	*Angel food cake cubes*
Maraschino cherries	*Vanilla wafers*

*Dip in lemon or pineapple juice to prevent discoloration of fruit.

CHOCOLATE-SOUR CREAM FONDUE: Substitute ½ cup dairy sour cream for ¼ cup of the half-and-half.

Frozen Rum Charlotte

Frozen Rum Charlotte

Chocolate Sauce (right)
17 *ladyfingers*
1/3 *cup rum*
3 *tablespoons water*
3 *cups chilled whipping cream*
1/4 *cup rum*

Prepare Chocolate Sauce; cool. Reserve 1 cup sauce. Cover and refrigerate remaining sauce.

Cut ladyfingers lengthwise into halves. Mix 1/3 cup rum and the water; dip cut surface of each ladyfinger half into rum mixture. Place ladyfingers, cut surfaces facing toward inside, on bottom and upright around side of springform pan, 9 × 3 inches. Beat whipping cream in chilled 2½-quart bowl until stiff. Mix reserved 1 cup Chocolate Sauce and 1/4 cup rum; fold into whipping cream. Spoon into pan; smooth top. Freeze until firm, about 8 hours.

Remove from freezer and refrigerate at least 1 hour but no longer than 2 hours before serving. Unmold Charlotte. Heat remaining Chocolate Sauce, stirring occasionally, just until warm. Cut dessert into wedges; serve with Chocolate Sauce. 12 to 16 servings.

Chocolate Sauce

1 *cup sugar*
1 *can (12 ounces) evaporated milk*
1 *package (12 ounces) semisweet chocolate*
  chips
1 *tablespoon margarine or butter*
2 *teaspoons rum*

Heat sugar, milk and chocolate chips to boiling over medium heat, stirring constantly. Remove from heat; stir in margarine and rum.

Chocolate Ice Cream

1 cup sugar
¹/₄ teaspoon salt
1 cup milk
3 egg yolks, beaten
2 squares (1 ounce each) unsweetened chocolate,
     cut into pieces
1 teaspoon vanilla
2 cups chilled whipping cream

☐ *For crank-type freezer:* Mix sugar, salt, milk, egg yolks and chocolate in 2-quart saucepan. Cook over medium heat, stirring constantly, just until bubbles appear around edge; cool to room temperature. Stir in vanilla and whipping cream.

Pour into freezer can; put dasher in place. Cover and adjust crank. Place can in freezer tub. Fill freezer tub ¹/₃ full of ice; add remaining ice alternately with layers of rock salt (6 parts ice to 1 part rock salt). Turn crank until it turns with difficulty. Drain water from freezer tub. Remove lid; take out dasher. Pack mixture down; replace lid. Repack in ice and rock salt. Let stand to ripen several hours. 1 quart ice cream.

☐ *For refrigerator:* Mix sugar, salt, milk, egg yolks and chocolate in 2-quart saucepan. Cook over medium heat, stirring constantly, just until bubbles appear around edge. Remove from heat; beat with hand beater until smooth; cool to room temperature. Stir in vanilla; pour into ice cube tray or loaf pan, 9 × 5 × 3 inches. Freeze until mixture is mushy and partially frozen, about 1¹/₂ hours. Beat whipping cream in chilled bowl until soft peaks form. Spoon partially frozen mixture into another chilled bowl; beat until smooth. Fold in whipped cream. Pour cream mixture into 2 ice cube trays or two loaf pans, 9 × 5 × 3 inches; cover to prevent crystals from forming. Freeze, stirring frequently during first hours, until firm, 3 to 4 hours. 1 quart ice cream.

ALMOND ICE CREAM: Stir in ¹/₂ cup chopped almonds and ¹/₂ teaspoon almond extract after adding whipping cream.

COOKIE ICE CREAM: Stir in 1 cup coarsely broken chocolate sandwich cookies after adding whipping cream.

NUT BRITTLE ICE CREAM: Stir in 1 cup crushed almond, pecan or peanut brittle after adding whipping cream.

PEPPERMINT ICE CREAM: Stir in ¹/₂ cup crushed wintergreen or peppermint candy sticks after adding whipping cream.

ROCKY ROAD ICE CREAM: Stir in ¹/₂ cup semi-sweet miniature chocolate chips, ¹/₂ cup chopped salted almonds and ¹/₂ cup miniature marshmallows after adding whipping cream.

EASY ICE CREAM DESSERT

Mocha Ice Cream Beverage: Let 1 quart vanilla ice cream stand at room temperature until slightly softened. Place ice cream in blender or mixer bowl with ¹/₂ cup chilled strong coffee and ¹/₄ cup chocolate-flavored syrup. Beat on high speed until blended or smooth. Serve immediately with cocktail straw and dessert spoon. 4 to 6 servings (about ¹/₂ cup each).

Ice-Cream Bombe

2 pints chocolate ice cream*
1 pint butter pecan ice cream
1 pint orange sherbet

Cut chocolate ice cream into 1-inch slices. Line bottom and side of chilled 1½- to 2-quart metal mold or bowl with slices; press firmly with spoon to form even layer. Freeze until firm, at least 1 hour. Repeat with butter pecan ice cream. Freeze until firm, at least 1 hour. Slightly soften orange sherbet. Press in center of mold. Cover and freeze until firm, at least 24 hours.

Unmold bombe on chilled serving plate. Return to freezer. Remove from freezer 10 to 15 minutes before serving to make cutting easier. Garnish with whipped cream, maraschino cherries, mandarin orange segments or mint leaves if desired. 8 to 10 servings.

*One of the following ice-cream combinations can be substituted.

Cherry ice cream, chocolate chip ice cream, chocolate ice cream.

Chocolate ice cream, French vanilla ice cream, coffee ice cream.

Peppermint ice cream, vanilla ice cream, chocolate ice cream.

Strawberry ice cream, pistachio ice cream, chocolate ice cream.

Sherbet Polka-Dot Dessert

2 pints lime sherbet
2 pints raspberry sherbet
2 pints orange sherbet
2 quarts chocolate chip ice cream
1½ cups chilled whipping cream
 ½ teaspoon almond extract

Working quickly, make balls of sherbet with small ice-cream scoop (#40) or teaspoon; place in chilled jelly roll pan. Freeze until balls are firm, about 4 hours.

Slightly soften ice cream; beat until fluffy. Layer sherbet balls in chilled tube pan, 10 × 4 inches, alternating colors and filling in spaces between balls in each layer with ice cream. Freeze until firm, at least 12 hours. (Dessert can be covered and frozen for several days.)

Beat whipping cream and almond extract in chilled bowl until stiff. Unmold dessert on chilled serving plate. Frost cake with whipped cream; return to freezer. Remove 15 to 20 minutes before serving to make cutting easier. 20 servings.

Spumoni Ice-Cream Loaf

1 pint chocolate ice cream
1 pint vanilla ice cream
¼ cup cut-up mixed candied fruit
1 teaspoon rum flavoring
1 pint pistachio ice cream

Line loaf pan, 9 × 5 × 3 inches, with aluminum foil. Slightly soften chocolate ice cream; spread in pan. Freeze until firm, at least 1 hour. Slightly soften vanilla ice cream; stir in fruit and flavoring. Spread over chocolate ice cream in pan. Freeze until firm. Slightly soften pistachio ice cream; spread over top. Cover; freeze until firm.

Invert pan to remove loaf; remove foil from ice cream. Cut into slices. 6 to 8 servings.

Frosted Ice-Cream Loaf

½ gallon Neapolitan, cherry or peppermint brick
    ice cream
2 cups chilled whipping cream
1 cup powdered sugar
½ cup cocoa
1 teaspoon vanilla
¼ cup diced roasted almonds

Unwrap block of ice cream; place horizontally on serving plate. Freeze until firm, about 4 hours.

Beat whipping cream, sugar, cocoa and vanilla in chilled bowl until stiff. Quickly frost sides and top of ice cream. (If ice cream starts to melt during frosting, place in freezer 15 to 20 minutes.) Freeze until firm, at least 3 hours. Just before serving, sprinkle top with almonds. 8 to 10 servings.

Mocha Topping

½ cup sugar
2 tablespoons cornstarch
⅛ teaspoon salt
1 cup cold strong coffee
1 square (1 ounce) unsweetened chocolate
2 tablespoons margarine or butter
2 teaspoons vanilla
1 cup chilled whipping cream

Mix sugar, cornstarch and salt in saucepan. Stir in coffee; add chocolate. Cook, stirring constantly, until chocolate is melted and mixture thickens and boils. Boil and stir 1 minute. Remove from heat; stir in margarine and vanilla. Cool.

Beat whipping cream in chilled bowl until stiff. Fold coffee mixture into whipped cream. Serve as a topping for angel food cake, chocolate cake or gingerbread. About 2½ cups.

Hot Fudge Sauce

Rich Chocolate Sauce

8 ounces sweet cooking chocolate or 1 package
    (6 ounces) semisweet chocolate chips
1/4 cup sugar
1/4 cup water
1/4 cup half-and-half

Heat chocolate, sugar and water in saucepan over how heat, stirring constantly, until chocolate and sugar are melted. Remove from heat; blend in half-and-half. Serve warm or cool. About 1 cup sauce.

Fudge Mallow Sauce

1/2 cup semisweet chocolate chips
20 marshmallows, quartered or 2 1/4 cups
    miniature marshmallows
1/3 cup half-and-half
1/4 teaspoon vanilla

Heat all ingredients except vanilla in saucepan over low heat, stirring constantly, until marshmallows are partially melted. Stir in vanilla. Serve warm. About 1 1/2 cups sauce.

COCOA FLUFF TOPPING

Beat 1/2 cup chilled whipping cream, 2 tablespoons sugar and 1 tablespoon cocoa in chilled bowl until stiff. Serve as a topping for desserts or pies. About 1 cup.

Hot Fudge Sauce

1 cup sugar
1 can (13 ounces) evaporated milk
1 package (12 ounces) semisweet chocolate chips
1 tablespoon margarine or butter
1 teaspoon vanilla

Heat sugar, evaporated milk and chocolate chips over medium heat, stirring constantly, until chocolate is melted and mixture boils. Remove from heat; stir in margarine and vanilla. Serve warm over ice cream. 3 cups sauce.

Glossy Chocolate Sauce

1 1/2 cups light corn syrup
   3 squares (1 ounce each) unsweetened
      chocolate, cut into pieces
   1 tablespoon margarine or butter
  3/4 teaspoon vanilla

Heat corn syrup and chocolate over low heat, stirring frequently, until chocolate is melted. Remove from heat; stir in margarine and vanilla. Serve warm or cold. 1 1/2 cups sauce.

Peanut Butter-Chocolate Sauce

Mix ¼ cup peanut butter, ¼ cup chocolate flavored syrup and ¼ cup corn syrup. Pour over vanilla ice cream. About ⅔ cup sauce.

Hot Bittersweet Chocolate Sauce

¼ cup margarine or butter
1½ squares (1½ ounces) unsweetened chocolate,
   cut into pieces
¾ cup sugar
¼ cup cocoa
¼ cup half-and-half
⅛ teaspoon salt
1 teaspoon vanilla

Heat margarine and chocolate in saucepan over low heat, stirring constantly, until smooth. Stir in sugar, cocoa, half-and-half and salt. Heat slowly to boiling; do not stir. Remove from heat; stir in vanilla. Serve warm. About 1½ cups sauce.

TOFFEE TOPPING

Refrigerate 3 bars (about ¾ ounce each) chocolate-covered toffee candy; crush bars. Beat 1 cup chilled whipping cream and ¼ cup sugar in chilled bowl until stiff. Fold in crushed candy. Serve as a topping for angel food cake, chocolate cake or gingerbread. About 2½ cups.

Crunchy Chocolate Sauce

Crunchy Chocolate Sauce

¼ cup margarine or butter
1 cup chopped walnuts or pecans
1 package (6 ounces) semisweet chocolate chips
½ teaspoon vanilla

Heat margarine in heavy skillet until melted. Add walnuts; cook over low heat, stirring constantly, until margarine is light brown; remove from heat. Add chocolate chips and vanilla; stir until chocolate is melted. Serve warm. 1¼ cups sauce.

DESSERT SAUCE TIPS

Chocolate dessert sauces are delicious served over vanilla, coffee, cinnamon or peppermint ice cream. For a quick dessert, top doughnuts or waffles with ice cream and drizzle with chocolate sauce. Or spoon over custard, rice pudding, gingerbread or unfrosted cake squares. Refrigerate any leftover sauce. To serve warm, reheat over low heat.

Candies & Snacks

1. Chocolate Apricots, 2. Three-minute Fudge, 3. Bourbon Balls

Old-fashioned Chocolate Fudge

2 cups sugar
²/₃ cup milk
2 squares (1 ounce each) unsweetened chocolate
   or ¹/₃ cup cocoa
2 tablespoons corn syrup
¹/₄ teaspoon salt
2 tablespoons margarine or butter
1 teaspoon vanilla
¹/₂ cup coarsely chopped nuts, if desired

Butter loaf pan, 9×5×3 inches. Heat sugar, milk, chocolate, corn syrup and salt in 2-quart saucepan over medium heat, stirring constantly, until chocolate is melted and sugar is dissolved. Cook, stirring occasionally, to 234° on candy thermometer or until small amount of mixture dropped into very cold water forms a soft ball which flattens when removed from water.

Remove from heat; add margarine and cool, without stirring, to 120° (bottom of pan will be lukewarm). Add vanilla; beat continuously with wooden spoon until candy is thick and no longer glossy, 5 to 10 minutes (mixture will hold its shape when dropped from spoon). Quickly stir in nuts. Spread mixture evenly in pan. Cool until firm. Cut into about 1-inch squares. 32 candies.

Nutty Mallow Fudge

1 package (6 ounces) semisweet chocolate chips
1 (4 ounce) milk chocolate candy bar
²/₃ cup marshmallow creme
1 tablespoon margarine or butter
1¹/₃ cups chopped nuts
1 can (5¹/₃ ounces) undiluted evaporated milk
   (²/₃ cup)
1¹/₂ cups sugar

Put chocolate chips, broken candy bar, marshmallow creme, margarine and chopped nuts into 2½-quart bowl. Heat evaporated milk and sugar in saucepan over medium heat, stirring constantly, until mixture boils. Boil, stirring constantly, to 225° on candy thermometer, about 5 minutes; remove from heat. Pour over ingredients in bowl. Stir until chocolate has melted and mixture is smooth and glossy. Pour into ungreased square pan, 8×8×2 or 9×9×2 inches. Cool until firm. Cut into about 1-inch squares. About 4 dozen candies.

Three-minute Fudge

²/₃ cup evaporated milk
1²/₃ cups sugar
¹/₄ teaspoon salt
2 cups miniature marshmallows or 16 large
   marshmallows, quartered
1¹/₂ packages (6 ounces each) semisweet chocolate
   chips (about 1¹/₂ cups)
1 teaspoon vanilla
¹/₂ cup chopped nuts

Butter square pan, 9×9×2 inches. Mix milk, sugar and salt in 2-quart saucepan. Heat to boiling over medium heat, stirring constantly. Boil 3 minutes, or until candy thermometer registers 225°, stirring constantly; remove from heat. Stir in marshmallows, chocolate chips, vanilla and nuts until melted. Pour into pan. Refrigerate until firm, at least 1 hour. Cut into 1½-inch squares. 3 dozen candies.

Easy Cocoa Fudge

1 cup granulated sugar
1/4 cup cocoa
1/3 cup milk
1/4 cup margarine or butter
1 tablespoon light corn syrup
1 teaspoon vanilla
1/3 cup chopped nuts
2 to 2 1/4 cups powdered sugar

Mix granulated sugar and cocoa in 2-quart saucepan. Stir in milk, margarine and corn syrup. Heat to boiling over medium heat, stirring frequently. Boil and stir 1 minute. Remove from heat; cool without stirring until bottom of pan is lukewarm, about 45 minutes. Stir in vanilla and nuts. Stir in powdered sugar until mixture is very stiff. Press in buttered loaf pan, 9 × 5 × 3 inches. Refrigerate until firm, about 30 minutes. Cut into 1-inch squares. 32 candies.

Rocky Road Fudge

1/4 cup milk
2 packages (5.75 ounces each) milk chocolate chips
2 cups miniature marshmallows
1/2 cup chopped nuts
   Dash of salt

Butter square pan, 8 × 8 × 2 inches. Heat milk and chocolate chips in 2-quart saucepan over low heat, stirring constantly, until chocolate chips melt; remove from heat.

Stir in miniature marshmallows, chopped nuts and salt. (The marshmallows will make little lumps in the candy.) Spread candy in pan. Refrigerate until firm, about 1 hour. Cut into 1-inch squares. About 4 dozen candies.

Soldier's Fudge

Soldier's Fudge

1 can (14 ounces) sweetened condensed milk
1 package (12 ounces) semisweet chocolate chips
1 square (1 ounce) unsweetened chocolate, if desired
1 teaspoon vanilla
1 1/2 cups chopped nuts, if desired

Butter square pan, 8 × 8 × 2 inches. Heat milk, chocolate chips and unsweetened chocolate in 2-quart saucepan over low heat, stirring constantly, until chocolate is melted and mixture is smooth; remove from heat. Stir in vanilla and nuts. Spread mixture evenly in pan. Refrigerate until firm, at least 1 hour. Cut into about 1 1/4-inch squares. About 3 dozen candies.

Truffles

6 squares (1 ounce each) semisweet chocolate,
   cut-up
2 tablespoons margarine or butter, cut into
   pieces
¼ cup whipping cream
1 package (6 ounces) semisweet or milk chocolate
   chips
1 tablespoon shortening (not margarine or
   butter)

Heat semisweet chocolate in heavy 2-quart saucepan over low heat, stirring constantly, until melted. Remove from heat; stir in margarine, then cream. Refrigerate, stirring frequently, *just* until thick enough to hold a shape, 10 to 15 minutes. Drop by teaspoonfuls onto foil-lined cookie sheet. Shape into 1¼-inch balls. Freeze 30 minutes.

Heat chocolate chips and shortening in double boiler or in bowl set over hot, but not boiling, water. (Water should not touch container.) Stir frequently until melted. Dip truffles, one at a time, into chocolate; place on waxed paper-covered cookie sheet. Sprinkle some truffles with finely chopped nuts immediately after dipping if desired. Refrigerate truffles until coating is set, about 10 minutes.

If desired, drizzle some truffles with melted chocolate or a mixture of ¼ cup powdered sugar and ½ teaspoon milk; refrigerate just until set. 15 truffles (about ½ pound).

ALMOND TRUFFLES: Stir 2 tablespoons almond-flavored liqueur into the cream before adding.

APRICOT TRUFFLES: Soak 3 tablespoons chopped apricots in 1 tablespoon brandy 15 minutes. Stir in after cream.

CHERRY TRUFFLES: Stir 2 tablespoons cherry brandy into the cream before adding.

ORANGE-FLAVORED TRUFFLES: Stir 2 tablespoons orange-flavored liqueur into the cream before adding.

Truffles

Granola Bonbons

2 cups powdered sugar
1½ cups granola (any flavor)
1 cup peanut butter
¼ cup margarine or butter, softened
2½ cups semisweet chocolate chips
    Finely chopped nuts or graham cracker
    crumbs

Mix powdered sugar, granola, peanut butter and margarine. Shape into 1-inch balls. Refrigerate until firm, about 1 hour.

Heat chocolate chips over low heat, stirring constantly, until melted. Remove from heat; place chocolate in pan over hot water. Dip bonbons into chocolate; immediately roll desired number of bonbons in nuts. Place on waxed paper-covered tray or cookie sheet. Store loosely covered in refrigerator. About 5 dozen candies.

Coconut Squares

2 tablespoons margarine or butter
2½ cups (7 ounces) flaked coconut
1 box (1 pound) powdered sugar (about
    4 cups)
¼ cup evaporated milk
½ cup semisweet chocolate chips

Butter square pan, 9 × 9 × 2 inches. Heat margarine in 2-quart saucepan over low heat until delicate brown. Remove from heat; stir in coconut. Stir in sugar and milk alternately. (Mixture gets very stiff; mix with fingers.) Press mixture into pan. Heat chocolate over low heat, stirring constantly, until smooth. Spread over coconut mixture; refrigerate until firm, about 1 hour. Cut into 1-inch squares. About 5 dozen candies.

Tips For Dipping Candy

Several kinds of chocolate can be used for dipping candy. Chocolate that contains a high percentage of cocoa butter requires special treatment in melting, called tempering, whereas compound chocolate, using cocoa and a vegetable fat other than cocoa butter, is simply cut up and melted. The recipes in this book usually specify semisweet chocolate chips or squares as they are readily available and are very easy to use. Some tips when dipping candy include:

1. Using a dry fork or fondue fork, dip the candy center or confection completely into the melted chocolate, one at a time. Lift up and draw the fork across the side of the pan or bowl to remove excess chocolate.

2. Place the candy on a waxed paper-covered cookie sheet or tray. Refrigerate candies just until coating has hardened, about 10 minutes.

3. Cover and store in a cool, dry place. Serve at room temperature.

4. If there is any melted chocolate remaining after dipping, it can be used to decorate tops of coated candies. Or stir in just enough nuts, raisins, coconut or cereal to coat, then drop the mixture by tablespoonfuls onto a waxed paper-covered cookie sheet and refrigerate until firm.

Peanut Butter Fudge

2 cups sugar
⅔ cup milk
2 tablespoons corn syrup
2 tablespoons margarine or butter
⅓ cup peanut butter
1 teaspoon vanilla
1 package (6 ounces) semisweet chocolate chips

Butter loaf pan, 9×5×3 inches. Heat sugar, milk and corn syrup in 2-quart saucepan over medium heat, stirring constantly, until sugar is dissolved. Cook, stirring occasionally, until candy thermometer registers 234°, or until small amount of mixture dropped into very cold water forms a soft ball that flattens when removed from water.

Remove from heat; add margarine and cool, without stirring, to 120° (bottom of pan will be lukewarm). Add peanut butter, vanilla and chocolate chips; beat vigorously and continuously with wooden spoon until mixture starts to thicken, about 1 minute. Working quickly, spread mixture in pan. Cool until firm. Cut into 1-inch squares. 32 candies.

Cream Cheese Fudge

2 packages (3 ounces each) cream cheese, softened
¼ cup margarine or butter, softened
1 teaspoon vanilla
¼ teaspoon salt
⅔ cup cocoa
1 pound powdered sugar (4 cups)
1 cup coarsely chopped pecans

Beat cream cheese, margarine, vanilla and salt on low speed until smooth. Beat in cocoa. Beat in powdered sugar, 1 cup at a time, until smooth. Stir in pecans. Press firmly in ungreased square pan, 8×8×2 inches. Refrigerate until firm, about 3 hours. Cut into squares about 1½ inches. Refrigerate any remaining candy. About 2 dozen candies.

Coconut-Chocolate-covered Cherries

2 cups powdered sugar
½ cup margarine or butter, softened
2 tablespoons cocoa
½ teaspoon almond extract
½ teaspoon vanilla
Dash of salt
1½ cups flaked coconut (about 4 ounces)
1 jar (10 ounces) maraschino cherries with stems, well drained*
⅓ cup finely crushed chocolate wafers

Mix powdered sugar, margarine, cocoa, almond extract, vanilla and salt; stir in coconut. Mold about 2 teaspoons mixture around each cherry; roll in wafer crumbs. Store in refrigerator. 2 dozen candies.

*1 jar (about 10 ounces) maraschino cherries without stems can be substituted for the maraschino cherries with stems. Mold 1½ teaspoons of the coconut mixture around each cherry. 3 dozen candies.

Banana Bobs

2 to 3 medium bananas
2 tablespoons shortening
1 bar (about 4 ounces) milk chocolate candy, plain or with crisped rice, cut up

Peel bananas and cut each into 3 or 4 pieces. Insert wooden ice-cream stick in each piece; place on cookie sheet. Freeze until bananas are firm, about 2 hours.

Heat shortening and chocolate candy in small saucepan over low heat, stirring occasionally, until melted. Remove from heat. Dip banana pieces into chocolate, quickly spreading mixture completely over pieces. Place on waxed paper-covered cookie sheet; freeze until firm. When firm, wrap each in aluminum foil and place in freezer. Remove from freezer 15 minutes before serving. 6 to 12 banana bobs.

Ting-A-Lings

Heat 1 package (12 ounces) semisweet chocolate chips or 12 ounces milk chocolate until melted. Stir gradually into 4 cups whole wheat flake cereal until flakes are well coated. Drop mixture by tablespoonfuls onto waxed paper-covered cookie sheets. Refrigerate until firm, about 2 hours. About 3½ dozen candies.

Chocolate Clusters

  1 package (6 ounces) semisweet chocolate chips
  ⅓ cup margarine or butter
 16 large marshmallows
  2 cups quick-cooking oats
  1 cup flaked coconut
  ½ teaspoon vanilla

Heat chocolate chips, margarine and marshmallows in 3-quart saucepan over low heat, stirring constantly, until smooth. Remove from heat; mix in oats, coconut and vanilla thoroughly. Drop by teaspoonfuls onto waxed paper. Refrigerate until firm, about 1 hour. 3½ dozen candies

NOTE: Chocolate, margarine and marshmallow mixture may separate but will hold together when coconut and oats are added.

BRAN-CHOCOLATE CLUSTERS: Substitute ½ cup whole bran cereal for ½ cup of the oats.

Haystacks

1 package (12 ounces) semisweet chocolate chips
1 cup Spanish peanuts
1 to 2 cups chow mein noodles

Melt chocolate chips in saucepan over low heat, stirring frequently. Stir in nuts and noodles until well coated; remove from heat. Drop by teaspoonfuls onto waxed paper. Refrigerate until firm. About 3 dozen candies.

Peanut Butter Bars

1¼ cups creamy peanut butter
 ½ cup margarine or butter, softened
  4 cups honey graham cereal, crushed
  2 cups powdered sugar
  1 tablespoon shortening
  1 package (5.75 ounces) milk chocolate chips

Mix peanut butter and margarine in 2½-quart bowl. Stir in cereal. Stir in powdered sugar, ⅓ at a time. Press mixture firmly in ungreased square pan, 9 × 9 × 2 inches.

Heat the shortening and chocolate chips in 1-quart saucepan over very low heat, stirring constantly, until melted and mixture is smooth. Spread chocolate over mixture in pan. Refrigerate until firm, about 1 hour. Remove from refrigerator 10 minutes before serving. Cut into bars, about 2¼ × 1½ inches. Refrigerate any remaining bars. 24 bars.

Bourbon Balls

  2 cups finely crushed vanilla wafer crumbs
    (about 50)
  2 cups finely chopped pecans or walnuts (about
    8 ounces)
  2 cups powdered sugar
  ¼ cup cocoa
  ½ cup bourbon
  ¼ cup light corn syrup
    Granulated sugar or chocolate shot

Mix wafer crumbs, pecans, powdered sugar and cocoa. Stir in bourbon and corn syrup. Shape mixture into 1-inch balls. Roll in granulated sugar. Refrigerate in tightly covered container several days before serving. About 5 dozen candies.

BRANDY BALLS: Substitute ½ cup brandy for the bourbon

Chocolate Taffy

1 cup sugar
³⁄₄ cup light corn syrup
²⁄₃ cup water
2 tablespoons margarine or butter
1 tablespoon cornstarch
1 teaspoon salt
1 teaspoon vanilla
1 package (6 ounces) semisweet chocolate chips

Butter square pan, 8×8×2 inches. Heat sugar, corn syrup, water, margarine, cornstarch and salt to boiling in 2-quart saucepan over medium heat, stirring constantly. Cook, without stirring, until candy thermometer registers 256° or until small amount of mixture dropped into very cold water forms a hard ball, about 20 minutes. Remove from heat; stir in vanilla and chocolate chips. Pour into pan; cool.

Cut into 1-inch squares. Decorate squares with nuts, shape squares into rolls, or mold squares around miniature marshmallows if desired. Wrap pieces individually in plastic wrap or waxed paper (candy must be wrapped to hold its shape). About 1 pound candy.

Peanut Butter Balls

1 cup powdered sugar
¹⁄₂ cup instant nonfat dry milk
1 cup crunchy peanut butter
3 tablespoons water
1 cup semisweet chocolate chips
¹⁄₂ cup graham cracker crumbs or flaked coconut

Mix powdered sugar and dry milk. Stir in peanut butter, water and chocolate chips. Shape into 1-inch balls. Roll balls in graham cracker crumbs until coated. Refrigerate until firm, at least 20 minutes. About 30 candies.

Chocolate-Coconut Drops

2 squares (1 ounce each) unsweetened chocolate
2¹⁄₂ cups (7 ounces) flaked coconut
¹⁄₂ cup chopped walnuts
1 can (14 ounces) sweetened condensed milk

Heat oven to 350°. Heat chocolate in 2-quart saucepan over low heat, stirring frequently, until melted. Remove from heat; stir in coconut, walnuts and milk. Drop by teaspoonfuls about 1 inch apart onto ungreased cookie sheet. Place in oven; turn off heat. Let stand in oven until candy has glazed appearance, about 15 minutes. Remove from cookie sheet while warm. About 4 dozen candies.

Fudge Meltaways

1³⁄₄ cups graham cracker crumbs (about 20 squares)
1 cup flaked coconut
¹⁄₄ cup cocoa
2 tablespoons sugar
¹⁄₂ cup margarine or butter, melted
2 tablespoons water
Frosting (below)

Mix cracker crumbs, coconut, cocoa and sugar. Stir in margarine and water. Press in ungreased square pan, 9×9×2 inches; refrigerate. Prepare Frosting; spread over crumb mixture. Refrigerate 1 hour. Cut into about 1-inch squares. Decorate with cut-up red and green candied cherries if desired. 60 squares.

Frosting

2 cups powdered sugar
¹⁄₄ cup margarine or butter, softened
2 tablespoons milk
1 teaspoon vanilla

Mix all ingredients until smooth. If necessary, stir in 1 to 2 teaspoons additional milk until of spreading consistency.

Creamy Chocolate Caramels

½ cup finely chopped nuts
2 cups sugar
¾ cup light corn syrup
½ cup margarine or butter
2 cups half-and-half
2 squares (1 ounce each) unsweetened chocolate

Butter square pan, 8 × 8 × 2 inches. Spread nuts in pan. Heat sugar, corn syrup, margarine, 1 cup half-and-half and the chocolate to boiling in 3-quart saucepan over medium heat, stirring constantly. Stir in remaining half-and-half. Cook over medium heat, stirring frequently, to 245° on candy thermometer or until small amount of mixture dropped into very cold water forms a firm ball. Immediately spread over nuts in pan. Cool; cut into about 1-inch squares. 3 dozen candies.

Chocolate Popcorn Balls

½ cup sugar
¼ cup margarine or butter
½ cup light corn syrup
2 tablespoons cocoa
½ teaspoon salt
8 cups popped corn (about ½ cup unpopped)

Heat all ingredients except popped corn to boiling in 4-quart Dutch oven over medium heat, stirring constantly. Stir in popped corn, Cook and stir until popcorn is coated, about 2 minutes; cool slightly.

Dip hands in cold water; shape mixture into 3-inch balls. Place balls on waxed paper; cool completely. 10 popcorn balls.

CHOCOLATE-PEANUT POPCORN BALLS: Stir in ½ cup salted peanuts with the popcorn.

Chocolate-Caramel Apples

6 medium apples
6 wooden skewers
6 tablespoons chopped nuts, if desired
1 package (14 ounces) caramel candies
¼ cup semisweet chocolate chips
2 tablespoons hot water

Insert wooden skewer into stem end of each apple. Place 1 tablespoon nuts in each of 6 mounds on waxed paper. Wash and dry apples, removing stems. Heat caramels, chocolate chips and water in top of double boiler over hot water, stirring frequently, until caramels are melted and mixture is smooth. Remove from heat. Keeping top part over hot water, dip apples into the chocolate-caramel sauce and spoon mixture over the apple until each is completely coated. Place each apple on a mound of nuts; turn each apple so it is coated with nuts. Refrigerate until caramel coating is firm, about 1 hour. 6 apples.

NOTE: If caramel mixture hardens while coating apples, melt over boiling water.

Easy Chocolate Confections

1 package (6 ounces) semisweet chocolate chips
1 tablespoon plus 1 teaspoon shortening
¼ teaspoon ground cinnamon, if desired
  Dippers (below)

Line jelly roll pan, 15½ × 10½ × 1 inch, with waxed paper. Heat chocolate chips, shortening and cinnamon in 1-quart heavy saucepan over low heat, stirring constantly, until smooth; remove from heat. Coat any of the Dippers (below) about ¾ of the way with chocolate mixture. Place in pan. Refrigerate uncovered until chocolate is firm, about 30 minutes. 3 to 4 dozen confections.

Dippers

Strawberries
Caramels
Dark sweet cherries
Maraschino cherries
Seedless grapes
Small pretzels or cookies
Large marshmallows

NOTE: Fruit should be dry before dipping.

WHITE CHOCOLATE CONFECTIONS: Substitute 3 squares (2 ounces each) white chocolate (vanilla-flavored candy coating), cut up, for the chocolate chips.

Marshmallow Bars

32 large marshmallows or 3 cups miniature
  marshmallows
¼ cup margarine or butter
½ teaspoon vanilla
5 cups crispy corn puff, toasted oat, corn flake
  or whole wheat flake cereal
1 package (6 ounces) semisweet chocolate chips

Butter square pan, 9 × 9 × 2 inches. Heat marshmallows and margarine in 3-quart saucepan over low heat, stirring constantly, until marshmallows are melted and mixture is smooth. Remove from heat; stir in vanilla. Stir

Easy Chocolate Confections

in half of the cereal at a time until evenly coated. Press in pan. Heat chocolate chips in heavy saucepan over low heat, stirring frequently, until melted. Spread over cereal mixture in pan; cool. Cut into bars, 2 × 1 inch. About 36 bars.

COCONUTTY-MARSHMALLOW BARS: Substitute ½ cup flaked coconut and ½ cup coarsely chopped nuts for 1 cup of the cereal.

PEANUT BUTTER-MARSHMALLOW BARS: Stir ½ cup peanut butter into marshmallow-margarine mixture until metled.

Easy S'More Treats

⅓ cup light corn syrup
1 tablespoon margarine or butter
4 bars (about 1.5 ounces each) milk chocolate,
  broken into pieces or 1 package (5.75
  ounces) milk chocolate chips
½ teaspoon vanilla
4 cups honey graham cereal
1½ cups miniature marshmallows

Butter square pan, 9 × 9 × 2 inches. Heat corn syrup and margarine to boiling in 3-quart saucepan; remove from heat. Add chocolate and vanilla; stir until chocolate is melted. Stir in cereal gradually until completely coated with chocolate. Stir in marshmallows. Press into pan. Let stand at room temperature at least 1 hour. Cut into bars, 2¼ × 1½ inches. Store loosely covered at room temperature for no longer than 2 days. 24 bars.

Chocolate Apricots

Heat ½ cup semisweet chocolate chips and 2 teaspoons shortening over low heat, stirring occasionally, until melted. Coat 24 dried apricot halves about ¾ of the way with chocolate mixture; place on waxed paper on cookie sheet. Refrigerate uncovered until chocolate is firm, at least 30 minutes but no longer than 24 hours. 24 apricots.

Index